John McLeod Campbell

Thoughts on Revelation

with special reference to the present time

John McLeod Campbell

Thoughts on Revelation
with special reference to the present time

ISBN/EAN: 9783337414016

Printed in Europe, USA, Canada, Australia, Japan

Cover: Foto ©Lupo / pixelio.de

More available books at **www.hansebooks.com**

THOUGHTS

ON

REVELATION

WITH SPECIAL REFERENCE TO THE PRESENT TIME.

BY

JOHN McLEOD CAMPBELL,

AUTHOR OF "THE NATURE OF THE ATONEMENT AND ITS RELATION TO THE REMISSION OF SINS AND ETERNAL LIFE."

Cambridge:
MACMILLAN AND CO.
AND 23, HENRIETTA STREET, COVENT GARDEN.
London.
1862.

THOUGHTS ON REVELATION.

GALATIANS i. 8.

"*But though we, or an angel from heaven, preach any other gospel unto you than that which we have preached unto you, let him be accursed.*"

It is thus that the Apostle writes to the Galatian Church, tempted to listen to false teachers, who perverted the gospel of Christ. No language could express more strongly the independent character of faith. Having received the truth, they were expected to hold it, with a confidence altogether irrespective of the channel through which they had received it: so absolutely so, that the Apostle's unsaying what he had taught, would not justify their ceasing to believe. Nay, if any supposable higher personal creature authority, that of an angel from heaven, were to commend another gospel, than that which they had received, they were to reject it. Not, of course, that the cases he puts were to the Apostle's mind possible cases; but his putting them is as instructive as if they were possible.

That which would be our security, if our faith were exposed to so extreme a trial as the Apostle supposes, belongs to the nature of true faith at all times, and ought to be our conscious peace under any ordinary trial to our faith, and, indeed, apart from all such trial: while it is a most important end of every trial of faith, to awaken into consciousness the elements of such peace, when, through lack of trial, they have ceased to be realized. How jealous the Apostle was on this subject, the whole tenor of his teaching testifies; which all accords with the view of the relation of teachers and taught, which he expresses when he says, "Not for that we have dominion over your faith, but are helpers of your joy: for by faith ye stand."[1]

It is in connexion with this subject, namely, the relation of the obligation of faith and of the sin of unbelief, to the inherent authority of truth, and the self-evidencing nature of light, that the "Essays and Reviews," and the discussions which

---

[1] 2 Cor. i. 24.

they have occasioned, have a real interest for us. Men now say that too much importance has been attached to this book—that the sensation it has produced has been unreasoning and foolish, and is fast dying away. Much of what has been felt may have been foolish: doubtless much has been so. So wide an interest could scarcely be, in all its extent, deep, or truly earnest. But, I believe, none of us can have passed through this discussion on the great subject of the divine authority of Revelation altogether unaffected by it—whether in the way of gain or loss.

There are three classes of persons, whose immediate feeling, in regard to whatever seems to them a questioning of the Divine authority of Revelation, we easily anticipate. 1. Those whose faith in Revelation rests on the assumed infallibility of the Church. 2. Those who have ceased to believe in Revelation. 3. Those who have a true faith in Revelation, being in the light of the truth which it reveals. It is natural that the first effect on each of these classes should be an increase of satisfaction with their own position: and we see that Superstition is clinging with more confidence to its blind faith, and that Infidelity is encouraged in its scepticism, while we cannot doubt that any trial of their faith, to which those who are abiding in the light of truth are finding themselves subjected, is strengthening to their faith. But we may hope, that the discussions which are raised, while a sure gain to this last class, may, eventually, be profitable to many of the other two classes also, through the clearing away of much of the mist of confused thought, on the subject of the divine authority of revelation, in which men too easily rest, but which is as alien to true faith as it is favourable to superstition and unbelief.

Nothing can contribute more to this desirable result, than increased simplicity and decision in taking that high ground, on the subject of faith, which we see the Apostle taking with the Galatians. Nor can we, standing on any lower ground, put forth the real strength of Christianity in its conflict with superstition and infidelity: while there are multitudes in whom a certain amount of superstition and infidelity are present only as alloys in a real Christianity, from which they may be delivered, by being forced to realize and rest only in that in their religion, which belongs to them as children of the light and of the day.

To descend here to ground lower than that which the Apostle takes is, in truth, to cease to be God's witnesses; for witnesses must speak what they know, and testify what they have seen. But in order to occupy intelligently that high ground which accords, and which alone accords, with our calling in Christ, we must consider our traditional faith, and assign to it its proper place and value.

Our traditional faith, we know, is what we are liable to be taunted with, at once by Infidels and Romanists; the former taunting us with calling that a faith in truth which, they say, is but a prejudice of education: the latter taunting us with virtually depending, as much as they do, on the Church for our faith; while denying to the Church that infallibility which alone can justify such dependence. "You believe in the Bible," say the former, "just as other nations believe in what are their sacred books. It is a mere accident of your birth, that your sacred writings are not the Koran or the Vedas, instead of the Bible." "You object," say the latter, "to our trust in the Church, our receiving the Scriptures as divine, simply on the authority of the Church; but what is the ordinary faith in the

Scriptures of any Protestant people, but a receiving them from the Church—the present living Church into which they are born? The young generation of each time, growing into intelligence, have the Bible put into their hands, as the Word of God, by that elder generation, from which they have sprung; nor is there any idea, on the part of the parents, of inviting their children to sit in judgment on the claim of the Scriptures to a divine origin. What they themselves hold them to be, as *that* they expect them to be received. We Romanists ask no more of our children; while we ask it on higher ground than you feel yourselves to stand on."

Let us, at once, admit what of truth is in this language. Let us recognize the presence of this traditional acceptance, as, at least, one element in ordinary faith in Revelation. This is in fairness due to Infidels and to Romanists alike, whose ears the refusal of a just concession will be sure to shut against us. It is also needful to the clear realization of our own position; that we may not put a higher price on our traditional faith than belongs to it, or lay more weight on it than it will bear. Otherwise, what might have been acknowledged, with intelligent thanks to Him of whose grace it is that we receive the Bible by tradition from our fathers, will be a hindrance to the development of true faith in us; and, it may be, cherish in us elements both of Infidelity and Superstition.

I say, "intelligent thanks to Him, a part of whose grace to us it is that we receive the Bible by tradition from our fathers." The fact of the tradition of error does not take from the value of the tradition of truth. This is not questioned when the tradition is simply moral: neither is it to be questioned when the tradition is religious. It is well when truth and honesty are presented to our opening intelligence, and our still undeveloped moral nature. It is well that they come commended by our parents, and with the prestige of parental authority. It is also well when the love of God, our Father in Heaven, and the manner of its manifestation in Christ, are early presented to our faith, and with the same sanction from those who themselves, in the very fact of their own relation to us, and of the love which belongs to that relation, are, at once, some illustration of what they teach, and a divinely appointed evidence of its truth.[1]

[1] Luke xi. 12.

But does the acknowledgment of the goodness of God here go to the length of justifying the taunt, that our faith is *merely* traditional? No, assuredly. The traditional element is not held to preclude or destroy the moral element, when the teaching is moral; and as little does it preclude or destroy the spiritual element when the teaching is spiritual. In teaching our children that which is in itself right, we are at once addressing and developing conscience in them; neither do we regard our teaching as successful, unless it awakens an independent sense of right; nor that we have taught our children to be true, unless they have a perception of the obligation and beauty of truth quickened in themselves. So also in our religious teaching, we realize the spiritual in our children, as we did the moral; making known to them the Father of their spirits, and then only feeling that our labour of love has truly profited them, when we see them worshippers, who worship God, who is a spirit, in spirit and in truth; for we know that the Father seeketh such to worship Him. Thus we occupy aright the place which God has assigned us in connexion with His gracious purpose for our children, namely, to reveal Himself to them.

But, while claiming for our traditional faith what is thus justly due to it, it is, at once, fair to objectors, and essential to the profitable consideration of our subject, to recognize the fact, that the independent faith of children of the light and of the day, required of the Galatians by the Apostle, is not the ordinary consciousness among us; nor even the recognized ideal of Christianity, of which it is our sin to be coming short. Knowing that the secret of the Lord is with them that fear Him,—is in truth limited to them by a moral and spiritual necessity, we cannot wonder that the traditional element should prevail in the ordinary faith of Revelation, considering how little men truly come to its light, or qualify themselves by experience for being witnesses for the self-evidencing nature of that light. But what is more difficult to understand is the undeniable fact, that men whose personal experience would seem to qualify them for taking this high ground, shrink from doing so. Most direct and immediate does their hearing of God in the written word seem to be. Their joy is as that of men seeing light in God's light. Yet when questions as to the ultimate warrant of faith in Revelation are raised, and Infidelity attempts to unsettle all faith, or Superstition attempts to place it on a false foundation, they seem to have no use of their own experiences, which are as unsuspected grains of gold in the ground on which men tread. Yet precious grains of gold these experiences undoubtedly are, and there is much need that attention should be directed to them, in order that they may be carefully gathered, and turned to proper account, in our Christian conflict. "This only would I learn of you, Received ye the Spirit by the works of the law, or by the hearing of faith?"[1] We are not lightly to esteem their labours, whose researches contribute to the clearness and certainty with which we receive the Scriptures, as having really the history which they are held among us to have—furnishing us with evidence that these Scriptures were written by those to whom they are ascribed, and at the time, and in the circumstances, and with all the supernatural accompaniments usually acknowledged. But it would be strange indeed, if the Bible is what we believe it to be, that it should not have a hold of our faith far other than this; that it should not, by virtue of what it is, have struck its roots deep into

---

[1] Galatians iii. 2.

our being, spreading infinite living fibres of these roots in our hearts and minds. To doubt this would be to doubt that it is the Word of God: and our great gain from anything that seems an attack on our faith, is to have the consciousness of these living fibres quickened in us. "For there shall arise false Christs and false prophets, and shall shew great signs and wonders; insomuch that, if it were possible, they shall deceive the very elect."[1] But false Christs deceive not the elect, *because they know the true Christ.* This suffices: nothing else could. Slight attacks on our faith may be dealt with on grounds that are outside, as respects our inner man; but trials to our faith may arise, for which nothing will prove the needed preparation, but that independent faith, that seeing light in God's light, even that experience of salvation, on which the Apostle's pleading with the Galatians proceeds.

Even while this is not recognized, writers on evidences give a certain place to that acknowledgment which the Bible has in the conscience of every man; and the records of personal religion abound in illustrations of the words, "He that believeth on the Son of God hath the witness

[1] Matt. xxiv. 24.

in himself."[1]   We also occasionally meet with seeming generalisations corresponding with this, as when Cowper says:

> "Conspicuous as the brightness of a star,
> Legible only by the light they give,
> Stand the soul-quickening words, Believe and live."

But all this comes far short of recognizing and avowing, in our defence of the truth, that claim for faith in its divine authority which belongs to the Bible on the ground of what it is. Nevertheless, in this must be found the ultimate justification of faith, the ultimate condemnation of unbelief.

Romanism is reproached with the "vicious circle," that the Bible is received on the authority of the Church, and the Church is trusted on the alleged authority of the Bible: but the same vicious circle is trod in other forms, and must be so until we see that Revelation is light, having the self-evidencing nature of light,—its claim to faith consisting in what it reveals. For to the question, "What is the faith due to Revelation, and on what does that faith ultimately rest?" this is the answer: God has spoken to us, and He expects that we are to know His voice: He has

[1] 1 John v. 10.

revealed Himself to us, and He expects that we shall recognize His glory, and say, "This is our God."

A true Revelation of God must be its own witness. It is not questioned that that prior and universal Revelation which God has given in creation and providence, shines by its own light. "The heavens declare the glory of God, and the firmament sheweth his handywork."[1] "The invisible things of Him from the creation of the world are clearly seen, being understood by the things that are made, even His eternal power and Godhead."[2] "He left not Himself without witness, in that He did good, and gave us rain from heaven, and fruitful seasons, filling our hearts with food and gladness."[3] How excellent this universal Revelation—how much more full of the light of life than we often realize it to be— we may understand, if we meditate on our Lord's comments on it: "Love your enemies, bless them that curse you, do good to them that hate you, and pray for them which despitefully use you and persecute you; that ye may be the children of your Father which is in heaven: for He maketh His sun to rise on the evil and on

[1] Ps. xix. 1.   [2] Rom. i. 10.   [3] Acts xiv. 17.

the good, and sendeth rain on the just and on the unjust."[1] "Consider the lilies of the field, how they grow; they toil not, neither do they spin: and yet I say unto you, That even Solomon in all his glory was not arrayed like one of these. Wherefore, if God so clothe the grass of the field, which to-day is and tomorrow is cast into the oven, shall He not much more clothe you, O ye of little faith?"[2] A part of God's prior-universal Revelation is the constitution of family life. The ordinance of parent and child reveals God as the Father of spirits; and therefore our Lord says: "If ye being evil know how to give good gifts unto your children; how much more shall your heavenly Father give the Holy Spirit to them that ask Him?"[3] Thus does our Lord recognize the Revelation that is in the divine system of things in which we find ourselves embraced, as a shining forth of divine light, its own witness, as it is the nature of light to be: for vision implies these two things only, namely, light, and an eye adapted to the light.

Illumination by the Scriptures has no lower character. "God, who commanded the light to shine out of darkness, hath shined in our hearts

---

[1] Matt. iv. 44, 45. [2] Ib. vi. 28—30. [3] Luke xi. 13.

to give the light of the knowledge of the glory of God in the face of Jesus Christ."[1] Accordingly the Apostle represents himself as, in preaching the gospel, " by manifestation of the truth commending himself to every man's conscience in the sight of God." Our Lord's own words are : " If I say the truth, why do ye not believe me?"[2] And thus we learn, from Him who is the Truth, this high attribute of truth, namely, to have its authority in itself, and to clothe with its authority him that speaks it. What the Apostle said of his own teaching, what our Lord Himself said of His, we may, so to speak, transfer to the Record of Inspiration as one whole. We are to regard it as commending itself to every man's conscience in the sight of God : that it speaks the truth is the condemnation of unbelief.

For the Bible is the unveiling of the divine procedure in the highest region to which man's thoughts can rise; recording divine acts, intimating divine motives, disclosing divine designs, shedding divine light on the past, the present, and the future of Man in his relation to God. All this the Bible claims to do. If, then, all this it does, we, standing in its light, are having our God

[1] 2 Cor. iv. 6.   [2] John viii. 46.

fully revealed to us; His name and His character declared and illustrated: the same which creation and providence revealed; but revealed here more fully, and in aspects going far beyond that prior Revelation, and therefore fuller of the light of the divine glory. If the more limited Revelation shines by its own light, how much more this!

If when I am asked, "How do you know that the Bible is a divine Revelation?" I thus answer, "Because it reveals God to me;" am I to be met by the further question, "How do you know that it is God that it reveals?" To such a question, the most solemn that can be addressed to a man, the answer is, that God is known as God by the light of what He is. If the Bible places me in that light, it makes me to know God, and to know that I know God with a pure and simple and ultimate certainty, to which no certainty in any lower region can be compared. "Whatsoever maketh manifest is light." Is this true of created light? Is it not in a far higher and the only absolute sense true of the uncreated light? "The city had no need of the sun, neither of the moon, to shine in it: for the glory of God did lighten, and the Lamb is the light thereof."[1]

[1] Rev. xxi. 23.

That is a solemn question which he puts who asks me, How, when I know God, I know that it is God I know? I must treat his question reverently, both because of its subject, and in tenderness to my brother who puts it; but I can only throw him back on his own question, and urge him to the deeper meditation of what it amounts to. Let him consider what would be implied in there being room for such a question. If God, presented to the faith of man as He is, is not to be identified by the light of what He is, is not the idea of "a Revelation" a contradiction, and faith an impossibility? This is the simple statement of what, as a moral and spiritual axiom, I see to underlie all reasonable demand for faith on the part of God,—all just condemnation of unbelief as resting on man. To any mere logical thinker, my understanding helps me to no further reply. To any earnest-minded brother, my heart's answer is, "How did the prodigal son know that it was his father that met him, while yet he was afar off, and fell on his neck and kissed him?" God in Christ reconciling the world unto Himself, not imputing their trespasses unto men, needs no witness but this glory of God in the face of Jesus Christ.

We, therefore, have gone quite astray, if, being in the full light of Revelation, we are asking for a witness to that light, external to itself; instead of receiving the light with the obedience of faith. Such obedience to light is due, because it is light,—simply on that ground. Whether it be the sun shining in the firmament, or the lily growing in the valley, or the sight of a father giving his son bread when he asks for it, and not a stone, by which I have the mind of my heavenly Father revealed to me, and am called to have faith in God—it is the light, that is thus shining on my spirit, that makes the faith called for reasonable, and unbelief a sin. If a heathen poet says, "We are God's offspring," it is that his word is true—a ray of light, that gives that word a claim to the response of faith. The greater fulness and clearness of light increases, proportionably, the obligation to faith, but it does not change the nature of that obligation. Can we recognize the justice of the condemnation because of disobedience to their comparatively dim and feeble light, pronounced by the Apostle on those who, "when they knew God, glorified Him not as God,"[1] and take lower

---

[1] Rom. i. 4.

ground in reference to the obligation to faith, which accompanies the possession of the Bible? That would be to reject the authority of the inspired comment which accompanies the record of the divine communications made to the chosen people. What was expected from them was but the opening of the eye to the divine light, of the ear to the divine voice. "Their eyes have they closed, their ears have they stopped;" this was the history of their unbelief, and its condemnation.

Gambold, in that prophecy of the time of the end with which he represents the early Church as comforting itself in the prospect of the "falling away first," speaks of "the sweet recovered infancy of faith:" and, doubtless, that word abides true, "Whosoever shall not receive the kingdom of God as a little child, shall in no wise enter therein."[1] Yet many give up the hope of a return to simple faith, as if this were now impossible. "Humanity," they say, "has developed beyond the stage at which men could receive truth as little children." But that is *a law of the kingdom of God* which is revealed to us in our Lord's words: "I thank Thee, O Father, Lord of heaven and earth, because thou hast hid

---

[1] Luke xviii. 17.

these things from the wise and prudent, and hast revealed them unto babes. Even so, Father, for so it seemed good in Thy sight."[1] We may not doubt that so it ever seems good in His sight. Nay, we may not doubt that here our Lord speaks out of His own consciousness, as God's Holy Child who could say, "I can of mine own self do nothing: as I hear, I judge."[2] The hearing of faith to which He calls us is a part of the example which He has set before us; or rather of the life of sonship which we have in Him.

Whatever elements of humanity have received a development, in our time, beyond what they had in Judæa, in the days of our Lord's life on earth; whatever we have inherited from Greece and Rome, in addition to what we have received through the nation to whom pertained the high distinction, that to them were committed the lively oracles of God; whatever Christendom has, in eighteen hundred years, produced of its own proper growth, over and above what it had inherited;—all which we, "the heirs of all the ages," are now either puffed up by, or humbly giving thanks for, for all gifts are susceptible of a right

[1] Matt. xi. 25, 26.   [2] John v. 30.

use, as well as of a perversion;—it remains true, and must for ever remain true, that the highest capacity of humanity is that which was manifested in the Son of God. No human consciousness can rise higher than His, as, here on earth, in feeble flesh, ever hearing the Father's voice He abode in His love, the well-beloved Son, as before His humiliation He was, and as in glory He is. Our birth so late into the world may make it to be true, that, in a certain sense, we come in for greatly accumulated riches of humanity; but Christ is the heir of all things; and the ages that have passed, and the ages to come, can yield no true and divine use of their riches to us, excepting in Him, in whom we receive an inheritance among them that are sanctified, and are heirs of God, being joint-heirs with Jesus Christ. However excellent and varied the good gifts with which God has endowed humanity, Christ remains God's Unspeakable Gift; above all gifts, inasmuch as He is Himself that true and proper life of man, in which alone any gift of God is enjoyed according to the divine purpose in bestowing it: for in the Son we have the life of sonship in which God is known as our Father, and His gifts as a Father's gifts.

We, therefore, are to regard the testimony of our Lord that we must receive the kingdom of heaven as little children, as a part of what the words include: "I am the way, the truth, and the life: no man cometh unto the Father but by me."[1]

Of the faith which receives the kingdom of God as a little child there is a counterfeit, which, though in truth its opposite, as darkness is the opposite of light, often passes for it, because it has a certain semblance of childlikeness and humility;—I mean the faith which is a blind submission to authority. This counterfeit faith seems childlike because it simply receives without questioning: it seems humble because the prostration of the mind under authority, not aspiring to any conscious discernment, has a certain semblance of humility: but with such seeming simplicity and humility, it is undeniably in this respect the opposite of that to which God's revelation of Himself is addressed, that it is no opening of a living eye to light, for which that eye is divinely adapted; no opening of the ear of the spirit to a voice whose self-commending tone of truth that ear is divinely formed to feel.

[1] John xiv. 6.

Therefore these two kinds of faith, whatever may seem to be common to them, are opposed as light and darkness are opposed.

But when we consider this counterfeit faith closely, we see that its seeming childlikeness is not really such; being no germ of sonship, no response to the drawing of the Divine Fatherliness, no trust of a spiritual and divine instinct reposing on the bosom of divine love. Infinitely higher is the instinctive security which the babe feels on its mother's breast, than this supposed transaction between us, God's offspring, and the loving Father of our spirits. And, as to humility, however such prostration of our intelligent being in the dark may seem humility, we know it to be altogether a counterfeit, when we compare it with that true humility which, in the light of what God is, and of what we ourselves are, with spiritual intelligence gives Him the glory that is due, and rests rejoicing in our own nothingness before Him.

The counterfeit faith which claims to be simple childlike believing, is seen in its most developed, and in a certain sense, self-conscious form, in Romanism. The Romanist receives the Bible as the word of God simply on the authority of the Church; and not only this, but, quite consistently, he further receives as authoritative the Church's interpretation of the Bible. Thus the Church interposes itself between us and God. We, God's offspring, are not to hear and know our Father's voice, nor to live a divine life in the light of His countenance. His felt Fatherliness is not to develope sonship in us; nor is the quickening of the life of sonship in us to raise us to communion with the Father. We are not to have communion with the Father and the Son in the Spirit. Kept at a distance from the living God, held incapable of hearing His voice, or seeing in His light, we are to be told about Him, and to believe in silence and in darkness.

How far back this is to go may not be very distinctly defined; but if we are thus incapable of direct communion with God and conscious dwelling in the light of truth, our dependence on the Church must in consistency go further. The Church must be our authority for believing that God is good, is holy, is righteous, is true, is love; yea, must be our authority for believing that God is. For as the Church interprets the Bible for us, so also must the Church interpret Nature and Providence, and the divine constitution of the Universe in which we find ourselves. The Church will thus be our authority for the faith "that the worlds were framed by the word of God, so that things which are seen were not made of things which do appear."[1] It will be our authority for seeing the Father's forgiving love,—that love which He calls on us to cherish towards each other,—in his "making His sun to rise on the evil and on the good, and sending rain on the just and on the unjust."[2] Nay, the feelings of our own hearts towards our offspring as these are a revelation of the heart of the Father of our spirits, must be interpreted for us by the Church, whose sanction we must have for believing that, "if we being evil know how to give good gifts unto our children, much more shall our heavenly Father give the Holy Spirit to them that ask Him."[3]

There is no limit to that surrender—that abnegation of all capacity of knowledge of God, which is implied in the claim of the Church to stand between us and God. Therefore when this claim is understood, the deep instinct of our spiritual being rises against it;—rises as a spiritual instinct of self-preservation against that

---

[1] Heb. xi. 3. [2] Matt. v. 45. [3] Luke xi. 13.

entire disinheriting of us as God's offspring to which it amounts; that hopeless distance from the Father of spirits, that outer darkness as proper to beings incapable of seeing light in God's light, that deep silence of the deaf as of the dead, as to all utterance of the divine love by the still small voice of the divine Spirit, to which it would consign us.

The divine excellence of Revelation is seen only when it is understood to be divine light, having the self-evidencing nature of light; and the true dignity of man is seen only when it is understood that he is divinely constituted in Christ with an eye adapted to that divine light. One and the same usurpation of the Church denies to Revelation the excellence of being light, and to us our birthright to be children of the light; in both ways withholding glory from God: for the light and the eye are both of Him, and together, and in their divine adaptation to each other, one work of God, one glory to God.

The great gain to us from fully realizing this ultimate result of the Church's interposition of itself between the individual man and God, will be the purging of our own faith in Revelation from any element that, under any other guise, tends to the same result. Therefore, when the Romanist charges us with holding the Bible by a traditional faith, which differs from his only in not resting on a divine warrant, such as his faith in the Church assumes, let us not evade the charge. Let us meet it frankly and fairly. Let us take the matter to the light of our calling to be " children of the light and of the day," "living epistles of the grace of God," " God's witnesses;" and whatever in our faith in Revelation will not approve itself in this light, let us at once acknowledge; permitting it to be called by its true name, and to be brought down to its true level. For we must stand forth, in the sight of our brethren whom we would deliver from spiritual bondage and a blind faith, as claiming to be in a better position than they, only in so far as in God's light we see light. We must do this if we would impart to them any sense of the superiority of that true and living faith which is obedience to divine light. Nay, we must do this even in simple fairness, if we would not unrighteously claim for a mere traditionary acknowledgment of the Bible, the value which belongs only to a true knowledge of the word of God. But what is thus due from us to others, that they may have confidence in our testimony as that of true men, is not less due to ourselves, that we may not, in this important matter, be self-deceived. We claim for Revelation the self-evidencing character of light. Do we ourselves honour Revelation according to the excellence which we thus ascribe to it? We vindicate our right as God's offspring to see light in His light. Are we exercising the high privilege for which we are thus jealous? Let us, as in the sight of God, press these questions home to ourselves, separating between our traditional and our living faith, and realising that the latter alone is what the Apostle contemplates' when he says, "By faith ye stand."[1]

The taunt that our faith is traditional, as it proceeds from Infidelity, is to be met in the same way as when it proceeds from Superstition; and, fairly dealt with, will be equally profitable in helping us to take true measure of our own position in reference to Revelation. In controversy with those who, admitting the existence of a divine Revelation, would interpose the Church between us and its light, we plead our relation to God as the Father of our spirits according to

[1] 2 Cor. i. 24.

the full knowledge of that relation which Revelation itself imparts. In controversy with those who reject Revelation, we plead the antecedent and independent faith of our relation to God as the Father of our spirits, as justifying our faith in Revelation as His gift. But still our pleading can only be from unfeigned lips in so far as we are children of the light for which we plead.

In the testimony of a heathen poet, that "we are God's offspring," heard as a voice from the depths of humanity, the Apostle, in philosophic Athens, found both a test and an argument,—nay, an axiom, from which to deduce the principle which must regulate the dealings of God with man, and the worship due from man to God. We are God's offspring: therefore he appoints the bounds of our habitation with the view of causing us to seek after Him and find Him, desiring that we should know Him in His nearness to us as the living God, in whom we live and move and have our being. This also is the explanation of such a dealing of God with man, as we recognise in the gift of Revelation: the Father of our spirits is seeking to make Himself known to us, and to bring us into communion with Himself. Here is a final cause; which, though such causes he regarded with distrust in mere science, is surely the most philosophic of all causes, when that which we are considering is the acting of Him who is not a fate or a necessity, but a living God, having a will to which moral attributes belong. We are God's offspring. He has for us a Father's love; the yearnings of the divine Fatherliness ever go forth towards us. Therefore has God revealed Himself to us, not only in measure by all in creation and providence which witnesses for Him, but fully by that Gospel of His Grace in Christ, in the light of which we know the divine Fatherliness which seeks to possess us as children, and the divine Sonship, in the fellowship of which we are to render to that Fatherliness the due and conscious response of filial love.

Therefore, in justifying our faith in Revelation, and in calling others to share in that faith, we bear ourselves as the offspring of God speaking to men, our brethren, of what is a part of the outcoming of the heavenly Father's love. Doubtless we owe it to any who find the faith of Revelation difficult, to approach this subject with them in the way that may help them most; starting with them from what we may reasonably expect them to recognize as the right starting-point. But we may not, in commending our faith, make any concession that virtually contradicts that faith. If when we assume that we are God's offspring, any would have us to take up as a previous question the Fatherliness, or even the very existence of God, we must contend for the recognition of both, as belonging to a healthy and right state of mind. If God is, and is our Father, and expects from us the honour and love due to a Father, what God has made us, and all His dealings with us, must accord with this. The faith which God expects from man, must have been contemplated and provided for in the constitution of man. That is equally a false and unrighteous tenderness to unbelief, which, in excusing man, would make God unreasonable,—one who would reap where he had not sown. "Without faith it is impossible to please God: for he that cometh to God must believe that He is, and that He is a rewarder of them that diligently seek Him."[1] That without which it is impossible to please God, must be reasonably due from man. The reasonableness of the demand for the faith that *God is*, is our

[1] Heb. xi. 6.

controversy with Atheism. The reasonableness of the demand for the faith that *God is a rewarder of them that diligently seek Him*, is our controversy with all forms of Theism that reject personal religion; refusing the recognition of a personal relation in man to a personal God. We cannot in either case concede the reasonableness of unbelief.

Both the elements of the faith without which it is impossible to please God, will have an indefinite expansion in us as our spiritual development advances. But in their essence, and as germs, they are proper to man, and reasonably due from all men. And this we see more and more clearly as our own spiritual vision strengthens.

That God is, is that ultimate and deepest truth of existence which we know only by faith, and in the exercise of that highest capacity of knowledge which faith is: for faith is not rightly opposed to knowledge, being the truest and most absolute knowledge. "The invisible things of God from the creation of the world are *clearly seen*, being understood by the things that are made, even His eternal power and godhead."[1] "Through faith we *understand* that the worlds

[1] Rom. i. 20.

were framed by the word of God; so that things which are seen were not made of things which do appear."[1] Is confidence more due to that lower part of humanity to which bodily vision belongs, which is common to us with the brutes, than to that highest part of our being which understands the relation of the visible to the invisible, and by reason of which, while looking at the visible creation, we clearly see the invisible eternal power and godhead of the Creator? Unwisely, though it may be with a true meaning, has it been said, "Knowledge is of things we see." There is a tendency to think of faith as in some sense a taking upon trust what we cannot directly know. But trust, to be justifiable, implies knowledge,—just that knowledge which is proper to faith; therefore the words are, 'clearly seen,' 'understand.'

But in the faith that God is, there is room for indefinite progress, from the dimmest spiritual instinct, which scarcely realizes itself, to the profound and assured sense of the Being of God, and that "on His Being our being reposes:" and the farther we advance in this faith, the more clearly do we see the original provision

[1] Heb. xi. 3.

for knowledge of God by which the divine demand for it is justified.

That God is a rewarder of them that diligently seek Him, is the second part in the insight of faith into the truth of things; its understanding of His meaning who appoints the bounds of our habitation that we may seek Him; its apprehension of personality in its own relation to Him in whom we live and move and have our being; its adding to the sense of our derived existence the consciousness that we are God's offspring, and not His creatures only.

And here also there is the same room for progress. The seeking which God rewards, grows from the darkest groping of the spirit feeling after the Father of spirits, on to the fulness of that life of sonship, in which entire devotedness of being responds to the demand, "Thou shalt love the Lord thy God with all thy heart, and with all thy soul, and with all thy mind, and with all thy strength."[1] The reward to them that seek God grows also as the seeking deepens in its character, up to the measure of the words, "Eye hath not seen, nor ear heard, neither have entered into the heart of man the

[1] Mark xii. 30.

things which God hath prepared for them that love Him."¹ And both the seeking and the reward, as we know more and more of them, shed light back on all by which from the first God has said to each of us, "My son, give me thine heart."

The elements of any knowledge are clearest and simplest to those who have themselves attained to the highest measure of that knowledge; and accordingly, He in whom faith was perfect, and in whom the knowledge of the relation of the human spirit to the Father of spirits was what belonged to the divine perfection of sonship in humanity, came to men honoring the Father in their sight, and making His doing so His claim on their reception of Himself,—their condemnation in rejecting Him. If He rebuked men for want of trust in divine providence, it was because He who clothed the lilies with beauty, and without whom a sparrow falls not to the ground, was *their Father;* and when He would ascend with men to the highest aspect of their relation to God, and would prepare acceptance for the revelation of redeeming love, the fountain of forgiveness to which He led them up was the

¹ 1 Cor. ii. 9.

divine Fatherliness. By the parable of the Prodigal Son, He meets, and we may say graciously condescends to, the difficulties of the Pharisees and Scribes when they murmured, saying, "This man receiveth sinners, and eateth with them."[1]

We, therefore, take the question of Revelation to the light of the Fatherliness of God, in which a divine Revelation is seen as an harmonious part of the love revealed, and what fitly finds a place in God's training of His offspring to be children of the light, walking in His light: only let us see to it, that in contending for Revelation on this ground we are consistent, and are not, by the condition of our own spirits, offering a practical contradiction to the enlightening power which we ascribe to Revelation, and because of which it is a gift worthy of God: for such a contradiction we exhibit if there remain any room for the imputation that we hold Revelation by a mere traditional faith.

Conscious dwelling in the light of truth is, doubtless, what alone can enable us to take the right ground in resisting any attempt to rob us of the Bible; whether that attempt take the

[1] Luke xv. 2.

form of coming between us and its light, or of denying its claim to be a gift from God. Yet such conscious dwelling in light is so little to be understood antecedent to experience, that, in commending it as our calling in Christ, we are exposed to much misconception, whichever form of error we have to deal with.

The controversial weapon often most relied on in contending for the infallibility of the Church, is the taunt, "Where is the grace of humility, if, trusting to your own individual judgment, you claim any certain knowledge of divine truth?" We know the tone of triumph with which this personal appeal is urged. "You rest on the infallible truth of Revelation. That is not questioned. But unless you are yourself an infallible interpreter of Revelation, how can you be sure that you understand the Bible aright? Knowing the infinite variety of opinion as to the meaning of Scripture, can you have the presumption to say that you stand with an assured confidence on the conclusions of your own individual judgment? Fallible as we individually are, we need an infallible interpreter; and that we do is itself a presumption in favour of the Church's claim to be such an interpreter."

The answer of faith is simple: "Our consciousness is not that of having formed an opinion. It is the consciousness of receiving divine light. In the light of God it would be not humility but untruthfulness to speak doubtfully of what we see. If learning of Him who is meek and lowly in heart, we are become in any measure the babes to whom truth comes with the seal of God, we may not intermingle any false and presumptuous show of modesty with our confession of what we believe. With the awe of divine truth and divine teaching on our spirits we believe and speak.

M. de Tocqueville, with philosophic insight, traced the comparative safety with which democracy was developing itself in America, to the high and pure conception of liberty entertained by the Pilgrim Fathers. "We seek," said they, "liberty; but not the liberty to do what we list, which is the liberty of a brute beast, but liberty to obey God unrestrained by men." So in regard to faith, we claim liberty, but not the liberty to think for ourselves, as if truth were matter of opinion, but liberty to hear God's voice and be taught of Him.

But here it is most important to be clear and

well-assured as to the ground on which we stand: for the right of free thought, when disconnected from the faith of divine teaching, and from the recognition of the self-evidencing character of divine light, while it repels the earnest Romanist whom we seem to invite from what he regards as sure ground, to take his place with us on the shifting sand of mere human opinion, exposes us defenceless to the Infidel; being such an admission of necessary uncertainty as is all the concession he will desire. The low ground taken in standing on a right of private judgment, irrespective of divine teaching, is altogether an error, and, when closely considered, is seen to be as much a coming down from the call to be children of the light and of the day, as the most absolute prostration of our minds before a Church claiming to be infallible would be. I know that this will seem a hard saying to many who yet will gladly echo all protest against the usurpation of the Church in dictating our faith. But if I must let go my hold of the promise, "They shall be all taught of God,"—the trust of the Psalmist, "In thy light shall we see light:" if the only alternative lies between an infallible Church and my own fallible judgment, I do not say that I shall be tempted to a blind effort to recognize a claim of infallibility which has no warrant, merely because it promises the comfort of an assured faith; I cannot so cheat myself. But how utterly cheerless is all that remains for me! The labour of forming opinions on which, when formed, I dare not lean: for the chances are incalculable against my being right, and all who differ from me being wrong. Surely I will say to myself, "Scepticism is forced on me; nay, is not the positivist after all, if this be so, the one who looks most fairly in the face the awful problem of existence? The sun shines in the firmament. I see it, and others see it also, and we walk together in its light. If, when I seem to myself to see in the spiritual firmament the Sun of Righteousness shining, and would walk in His light, any one is entitled to say that in this I may deceive myself—that *he* does not see it, that therefore, for all *I* can be sure of, there may be no such sun—where am I? Nay, I bless God that in the light of Christ I may and must answer—that the eye with which I see this divine light belongs to what is deepest and surest in my being; that I could more easily doubt the shining of the material sun in the firmament, more easily believe that all this visible universe was a phantasm, than doubt the reality of what my spiritual vision apprehends. And, whereas if a blind man should say, "I do not believe in the existence of light; it has no existence to me;" I should feel no misgiving as to the light of day, though I had nothing to oppose to the blind man's scepticism but the testimony that came to him from without, my own and that of others; in the case of the man who says to me, "I do not believe in the spiritual light you speak of; it has no existence to me," I should have this additional confidence in dealing with his scepticism, that I know and am assured, that the light of life in which I am seeing, is shining in him also—is present in his darkness, though the darkness is not comprehending it. To bring light to the physically blind, is hopeless; there is no power in the sun's ray to quicken into life the dead nerve: but it is never hopeless to present light to the spiritually blind. In hope, by manifestation of the truth we commend ourselves to every man's conscience in the sight of God.

When we claim to see light in God's light,

the Infidel is as intolerant as the Romanist. That which we are contending for is in truth the birthright of humanity; and therefore those with whom we contend have the same interest in our being in the right which we have ourselves. But they do not see this; and we risk having the true character of our position misapprehended, nay, of awakening impatience, and what Gambold calls "the anger of sick minds." No largeness in our faith, no assertion that the light in which we walk is the light which lighteth every man, that the voice to which we are giving heed is that which addresses every heart, saying, "Hear and your soul shall live," will save us from the charge of arrogating something to ourselves. The humble, lowly attitude of waiting on the divine teaching is not understood; the claim to enjoy that teaching is alone considered: and this is called presumption. The divine light may be revealing our own nothingness as we never knew it before; the consciousness that the light which is dawning on us in God's light may be overawing us; we may be realizing all the solemn difference between being taught of God, and leaning to our own understanding; our incipient faith, also, may be accompanied with the most self-condemning sense of the sin of previous unbelief; nay, the faintness and feebleness of our faith now, may be giving to our inward response to God the tone of his words who said, "Lord, I believe; help thou mine unbelief;"—this may be the truth of the case as respects our own consciousness, and yet the imputation of arrogance and presumption, and of thinking ourselves special favorites of heaven, may be our aspect from the stand-point of brethren, to whom we are, if they would listen, witnesses for our and their Father in heaven; witnessing for that nearness to Himself, and communion with Him in the light of life, to which they, as we, are called in Christ.

The assured possession of the truth must necessarily humble; and it must also secure a due reverence for conscience in others. The light in which a man can no longer call man master, is light in which he can no longer desire to be called master. There is nothing as to which there is more self-congratulation among us, than the progress men are assumed to have made in the true understanding of religious toleration. This the due recognition of the right of private judgment is supposed to have secured.

And here we of this generation compare ourselves with the Reformers, greatly to our own advantage. At first sight nothing can look more inconsistent than the conduct of the Reformed Churches; persecuting in their turn their persecutors, and then persecuting one another. As to this seeming inconsistency, it must be remembered that it was not of the use of power on the part of the Church of Rome to enforce *conformity* that the Reformers complained, but of that use to enforce conformity to *error*. The same use of power they were therefore ready, and without inconsistency, to justify, and practise in the interest of truth. It was a prejudice of their education, an error which they took with them out of the Church of Rome, to think that the knowledge of truth conferred a right so to act, or that the interests of truth could at all be thus promoted. This was their error, from which a more enlightened apprehension of the position of man as the subject of the divine teaching would have delivered them. He who is tolerant because he dare not interfere with what is God's province, is tolerant on the highest ground: and his toleration will not fail. Believing that the Father of the spirits of all flesh is dealing with men, His offspring, seeking to make Himself known to them; believing that in this He is exercising judgment and mercy, blending both according to that knowledge of what is in man which is exclusively His own; hiding things from the wise and prudent and revealing them to babes; yet often bringing it to pass that the wise and prudent of yesterday is the babe of to-day;—so believing, we must needs refrain from judging. We see all nature, all providence, all revelation, used in subordination to the drawings of the Holy Spirit of God, according to that divine constitution of things in Christ, which our Lord's words recognise: "All things are delivered unto me of my Father: and no man knoweth the Son but the Father; neither knoweth any man the Father save the Son, and He to whomsoever the Son will reveal Him."[1] Who, having this faith, can dare to interfere and say when, and how, and to what extent, his brother man is rebellious to light, and guilty in respect of unbelief; or attempt to single out for censure the wise and prudent who lean to their own understanding; or to apportion the praise due to the babes who are receiving the kingdom of God as little children?

[1] Matt. xi. 27.

True pure toleration towards others is as sure an accompaniment of being consciously taught of God, as humility is to ourselves. How clearly in our own case does the light which is humbling us under the mighty hand of God, justifying His judgments while revealing His mercy which endureth for ever, shew us how little others could have done us justice, either in blaming or encouraging! How much they must ever blunder, if they make the attempt, however disposed to deal fairly by us! Oh! how would their patience have failed where we most needed patience—how far short of the forgiveness called for would their forgiveness have been, and yet how much less at other times has our sin been than their estimate of it! How much has there been to justify the mercy shewn to us, in that we did ignorantly in unbelief that which we did amiss, although that unbelief also was sin. Nay, have there not also been days of small things in our inner history, which God has not despised though men might? What we thus feel to be the unfitness of others to mete out justice to us, we feel is our own unfitness to mete it out to others. We therefore judge not; but rather give thanks that they, as we, have to do with

Him who "will not break the bruised reed, nor quench the smoking flax, until he bring forth judgment to victory."

But the toleration which is the reverent recognition of God's exclusive judgment in all that concerns the history of His own dealing with the spirits of men, and their acceptance or rejection of divine light, is in no way to be confounded with that toleration which leaves the divine teaching out of account, and recognizes a right in every man to determine for himself what he shall hold as truth; which is essential infidelity as to the fixed and unchanging nature of truth, and the will of God that we shall know it.

In so far therefore as the toleration on which we now congratulate ourselves, and which seems so great an advance since the Reformation, is of this latter character, it is quite deceptive. The stern zeal for truth of the Reformers, however unenlightened, was a higher thing than the liberalism that is tolerant of all opinions because it has no real faith in truth, or, at least, in its attainableness by man. Such tolerance has no righteous root, and therefore easily passes into intolerance. For, just as Democracy becomes

Tyranny when the will of the many overbears the right of the few; so, seeming freedom of thought, and the putting of all opinions on a level, becomes the taking away of the right of private judgment when public opinion overbears the convictions of individual men. A right higher than the will of the many, a truth above opinion, must be recognized, if there is to be true liberty or true toleration. That seeming toleration which is essentially infidel may not be trusted. It bears the same relation to Infidelity, that the demand for blind faith does to Superstition : and it may yet be, that in its full development, the one shall bear fruit as bitter as the other has ever borne. The faith which responds to God's teaching, and calls no man master, may be as severely tried by a tyrant democracy enforcing conformity to public opinion, as it has been by despotic power doing the bidding of a Church claiming to be infallible. But this can only be if the religious element in the toleration we now enjoy, and for which we give God thanks, be unhappily overborne by the infidel element; and reverence for conscience, and faith in the teaching of God, give place to a manner of self-assertion which shuts out God.

There is one class of persons among those who do not acknowledge Revelation, whose system might seem to necessitate toleration,—I mean those whose theory of humanity rests on the principle of development. As the assumed subject of a process of development, each step in which has its necessary causes in previous conditions, man must be entitled to toleration of the most absolute kind. Our faith in Christ calls us to toleration, in fellowship with that long-suffering patience in God, of which we ourselves as well as all others are continual monuments. But *that* toleration should be something more absolute still, which belongs to a system which leaves no room for long-suffering at all; rendering impatience with evil in any form as unreasonable as impatience with the earlier stages of development in any physical growth. In this system the tree of humanity is seen growing and expanding as one great entity. The successive generations of men come forth and die down as leaves,—their virtues and vices, their glimpses of light, their wanderings in darkness, as well as all their joys and their sorrows, but the gleaming in the sunshine, or the shaking in the wind, of these

E

leaves,—until they successively wither and fall, having, it is assumed, served the end of their being, in contributing to the growth of that great tree to which they belong. The philosophic calm in which man is thus regarded, may not, without denying its nature, be disturbed by the excitement of occasions for praise or blame, or be visited with any temptation to intolerance. Yet the selfish pride of system may shew itself as powerful, and be as easily irritated by contradiction, in the case of this new error, as in that of the older errors which it seems to be supplanting; while an instinctive sense of deadly opposition from the truth ever haunts error, and moves it to intolerance, whatever its theory on the subject of toleration may be : and no form of error has more cause to fear this opposition than the system which substitutes a spontaneous self-development of humanity, for a divine education of man as the offspring of God.

Whether as a form of Atheism, or a Pantheism, or a Theism leaving a place for a Personal God, but removing Him to an infinite distance from us, and our hearts, and our lives, the system of development is altogether subversive of religion; *i. e.* of the sense of a personal relation of man to God, to which belongs intercourse and communion. Above all it is the extreme opposite of Christianity, that life of sonship in the Son of God, in which the full consciousness of our relation to the Father of our spirits is to be known in a personal communion of love; God's love embracing us personally, and responded to in the free personal devotion of our whole being to Him.

To this life we attain by a faith which has in it painful elements, doubtless; for our Saviour is He who came to seek and to save that which was lost. The knowledge of the redemption which we have in His blood, even the forgiveness of sins, involves the knowledge and confession of our sins; and there is no human consciousness more painful than the consciousness of sin. When that is really quickened in us, it takes all the comforting and sustaining power of the faith of forgiveness, and of the prospect of being saved from sin, and spiritually healed, to uphold the self-reproaching spirit, which otherwise would sink in hopeless remorse. And this pain is what the theory of development would spare us; promising a bright future, while shedding no condemning light on the past.

But we know the price at which this immunity from the pain of confessing sin would be purchased. And we would not exchange even the most condemning remembrance of our rebellion against the Divine Will, for the faith of the syren song, that the idea of rebellion to the Divine Will is a delusion, that we neither have been, nor could be, other than the necessity of our being determined. Such a theory of humanity we feel would degrade man from the dignity of that free relationship to God, which even man's abuse of it in sin proves; and to which belongs all capacity of redemption, and all hope of holiness, and of a free choice of the will of the Holy One. For to eliminate from the history of the race, or of the individual, all actual resistance of the human will to the Divine Will, is to reject the light of conscience, as well as of Revelation, and is as repulsive in its issues, as it is impossible without violence to that in our conscious being which we must most reverence.

Much, doubtless, of most humbling, painful feeling would be spared to us, if our progress in moral and spiritual illumination could be like our progress in any science or art; and the light and acquisition of to-day cast no blame on the darkness of yesterday: but this, in this region, would, we know, be a contradiction. To see that it is right to love God and to love man, is to see that it was wrong, blame-worthy, a thing for which to condemn ourselves, ever to have been otherwise minded. We cannot deny our own moral nature to escape its responsibilities: we would not if we could; for this would be to forego its hopes.

And with the loss of ourselves in respect to what gives its true value to existence, would come the loss of our God—of God as we know Him and love Him. All that we have acknowledged as long-suffering mercy would pass away from our faith. The love in God that commends itself to us in that while we were yet sinners Christ died for us, would become meaningless; and the love quickened in us, loving much because we believed much to be forgiven us, would have its fountain dried up. Our earthly lispings of the praises of redeeming love would be silenced, and there would be no place in eternity for the song round the throne, ascribing " glory and dominion for ever and ever" " unto Him that loved us and washed us from our sins in His own blood, and hath made us kings and priests unto God and His Father."[1]

Such would be the price of immunity from the pain of a true and living confession of sin; pain justly due from us sinners, yet from which we not the less shrink, even when no doubt is cast on the authority with which conscience condemns; so that a theory which denies that authority may be to us a temptation. This however only if we forget or understand not the place which confession of sin has in the history of our redemption: for in drawing back from this bitter but wholesome pain we refuse our part in the words, "He bare the sin of many, and made intercession for the transgressors;"[2] so that God cannot in our case be known as "faithful and just to forgive us our sins and to cleanse us from all unrighteousness." That is the path of life, at the entrance of which this necessity for the confession of sin meets us. Unless we know what it is to be reconciled to God by the death of His Son, we cannot know what it is to be saved by His life. Therefore, immunity from the sense of sin involves the loss of the whole "hope of our calling;" and the system

[1] Rev. i. 5, 6. [2] Isaiah liii. 12.

of which such immunity is the commendation would, were it the truth, as with the wand of a magician, convert into dross our unsearchable riches in Christ, God's precious thoughts for us which are more in number than the sand of the sea-shore.

What is thus subversive of Christianity, while not a mere scepticism, but offering something in place of what it would take away—a hope for man though not an anchor of the soul entering in within the vail—" another Gospel which is not another"—must, if it have any vitality, be animated in no ordinary measure by the antagonism of error to truth ; too much so for the control of mere consistency; while there is no aspect of Christianity which it is more likely to regard with intolerant impatience than the place which Revelation has in our faith. But such impatience may not overcome our fellowship in the divine love to men and our hope in God for them " according to the working whereby He is able even to subdue all things unto Himself."

I have dwelt so much on the relation of true humility as to ourselves, and true toleration as to others, to the consciousness of being taught of God, desiring to remove a prejudice against that consciousness as a part of the ideal of Christianity. But no toleration inconsistent with the recognition of the fixed and certain character of truth, and of the moral obligation of faith in God, can be a part of the love we owe to others, any more than it could of love to God. If then on these points anything is expected from us which we cannot concede, let us, as to the first, remember that we can only allow to others the measure of liberty which we have for ourselves; as much, and no more. In the higher region of spiritual truth, as in the lower region of science, man creates nothing, causes nothing to be. He is simply occupied in learning to know what is. It is therefore as unreasonable to expect us to treat truth as a matter of opinion in the one region, as it would confessedly be to do so in the other. And as to the second point, we know the Apostle's counsel, "Take heed, brethren, lest there be in any of you an evil heart of unbelief in departing from the living God;"[1] and our Lord's command, "First cast out the beam out of thine own eye; and then shalt thou see clearly to cast out the mote out

---

[1] Heb. iii. 12.

of thy brother's eye;"[1] and the more we understand the root-place which faith in the living God has in our spiritual life, the more shall we see that if any one evil in us be more especially the 'beam' which our Lord contemplates, it must be that evil heart of unbelief against which the Apostle warns us. Nor shall we wonder that the same evil is represented by our Lord as a beam in the individual's own consciousness, and a mote as seen in another. For this accords with that intimate knowledge which we are expected to have of the dealings of God with our own spirits, and of our own resistance and slowness of heart to believe; while the corresponding history in others is hid from us: and though we might conclude from analogy that their history in this respect is more or less like our own, we know that a deep sense of evil in one's own case always awakens the feeling that it is almost impossible that the case of another can be equally bad. There is no affectation or false humility in the language of the Apostle, when he speaks as feeling himself to be less than the least of all saints. But though in the lively sense of all by which God is revealing Himself to me, and

[1] Matt. vii. 5.

drawing me to Himself, unbelief in myself is rightly to me as a beam, and unbelief in another but as a mote in comparison; self-knowledge and the experience of deliverance, while fitting me for the loving service of taking the mote out of my brother's eye, obliges me at the same time to identify it with the beam in my own eye.

Since faith in God is a response to a revelation which is general, and not special, we cannot justify our own faith without condemning the unbelief of others. Would not our hearts misgive us if the witness for God which this fair universe is to us, the heavens declaring His glory, and the earth shewing forth His handywork, were heard as a witness to *us* and not to *man?* If the commendation of the Gospel to our conscience were not recognized as its just commendation to every man's conscience in the sight of God, could it continue sure to us? He who is ready to complain of us in this matter, saying, "Believe as you will, but do not disturb me in my opinions, or doubt that these may be as good for me as yours for you;" considers not that our belief about ourselves is our belief about him also. The drawings of divine love to which we feel it blessedness to yield would immediately be felt to be a fond dream if they were discovered to be something individual to us, and not the mind of God towards man.

There is at this moment no practical question more difficult or more delicate, than this of the true ground to be taken with unbelief. Two things are clear, we are not to fail in brotherly love, and we are to be true to the Truth. But we cannot doubt that practically these are one. We can only, in our care for others, hope to be profitable to them in the measure in which our dealing with them is according to the truth of things; that is, in this case, the truth of their personal relation to God. All our endeavours to enlighten others are in subordination to the teaching of the Spirit of truth, to whom it belongs to guide into all truth; but whatever is done in this subordination, must be one with what we know to be the teaching of this Divine Teacher. We may meet such questionings of unbelief as these: "We know that God is; but how do we know that we stand to Him in any personal relation of loving interest, such as speaking of Him as a Father, and of men as His offspring, implies? We owe existence to Him; but is it not an unwarranted transference of human feelings to the Divine Being to ascribe to Him a special interest in us, imagined after a human type?" Or beyond this: "We know that this universe exists, but how do we know that its existence is to be traced to the will of a Being such as we fancy to ourselves, and call God?" If such questions are urged we must answer according to our faith—the faith that God is not leaving Himself without a witness to the questioners, that He is witnessing to them that He is, and also that He is their Father. To act otherwise would be as if a geometrician were to give up the axiomatic character of his axioms, and let their truth be held an open question.

Dwelling much on arguments for the being and attributes of God, has undoubtedly a tendency to weaken our sense of the moral obligation of faith in God; and resting in a mere traditional faith has the same tendency. Yet the confidence inspired by triumphant argument, and the traditional habit of faith, are alike found to generate an unloving and self-righteous feeling towards all forms of Infidelity. The intolerance which has this origin repels us: more especially if we are ourselves earnestly engaged with that which is the real question between man and his

God, namely, the obligation for actual faith in the living God, the opposite of the evil heart of unbelief. For we see that as to this question, the mere triumphant arguer and the mere holder of traditional faith may not be nearer to the divine requirement than the Infidel; so that their self-congratulations are unwarranted, and their attempts to deal with error necessarily wanting in wisdom. They have not cast the beam out of their own eye; therefore they cannot see clearly to cast the mote out of their brother's eye. Nevertheless, the moral obligation of faith is clear, and we must feel constrained to contend for it, if we have awakened to the sense of that moral obligation ourselves. The Apostle says, "without faith it is impossible to please God." If he had said that without truth, or without righteousness, or without brotherly love, it is impossible to please God, many would at once assent, who cannot freely respond to what he does say. Yet what he does say is most sure, and has a clear response in conscience. "Thou shalt love the Lord thy God with all thy heart, and with all thy soul, and with all thy mind, and with all thy strength: this is the first commandment; and the second is like, namely this, Thou shalt love thy neighbour as thyself."[1] The second is like the first, indeed flows from it; and can be truly understood only in the light of the first, or truly obeyed only through that root-deliverance from self which is experienced in obeying the first in spirit and in truth. We cannot call any man our brother in the truth of brotherhood, until we have learned to call God Father in the truth of sonship. We learn both in the light of Christ, the Son of God, and the Brother of every man, in whom we have the life of sonship and of brotherhood. "Love your enemies, bless them that curse you, do good to them that hate you, and pray for them which despitefully use you and persecute you; that ye may be the children of your Father which is in heaven."[2] We cannot successfully urge the obligation to love our neighbour, of which these words of Christ express the extreme demand, without recognizing that obligation to love God which is prior and deeper—the root-obligation; and in so doing recognizing the obligation of the faith which love presupposes.

As to actual unpreparedness in any to respond to the demand made for God, *that* we meet also

---

[1] Mark xii. 30, 31. [2] Matt. v. 44, 45.

as to the demand made for man. We have often to speak of right and wrong, and the duties man owes to man, to persons in whose case the attempt to awake a response seems almost hopeless. Yet we do not therefore permit a doubt as to the authority of conscience, or the eternal distinction of right and wrong, or the living presence of conscience in these persons themselves, however it may seem asleep; and so we set ourselves, in the words of Coleridge, to "rouse the virtues that are dead in no man." Is the attempt more hopeless when we speak to men of God their Father, than when we speak to them of men their brethren? When the prodigal "came to himself" his first thought was of his father, his first true self-consciousness that he was a son, though not worthy to be called a son.

Our Lord's coming to men always in the Father's name has been already urged as guidance for us. When He says, "I am come in my Father's name and ye received me not," He adds, "if another shall come in his own name, him ye will receive." The evil state of the heart manifested in refusing Him who came in the Father's name, was to shew itself out fully in the welcome which would be given to one coming in his own name: by which I understand coming in the name of humanity, asserting the self-sufficiency of man, and so denying God, making man a God to himself. Christ said, "I am the light of the world;" He also said, "Ye are the light of the world." His gospel ministered by us will *prove* men as His personal ministry did. We may not attempt, by a lower demand as to faith, to win a readier attention, or hope to make a way for God into the hearts of men, otherwise than by presenting Him to their faith as He is revealed in the Son who comes to them in the name of the Father.

I know that many who are capable of much tenderness in their dealing with ordinary sin, or even with extreme moral degradation, have yet to learn how to deal with unbelief in the strength of love. While on the other hand others go to the opposite extreme of a tenderness and indulgence to doubt, which would make God's demand for faith less reasonable, less righteous, than His demand for moral goodness. Both errors I believe have one root; namely, not discerning the moral nature of faith in God. Not discerning this, not seeing faith in the living God as the *due* response to His manifestation of

Himself to our spirits, faith is confounded with orthodoxy of creed; and those who take dogmas on trust naturally fall into the first error; and those who are much occupied with the history of opinions, or much exercised with mental difficulties, fall into the second. Nothing can so tend to set all this right as deliverance from a mere traditional faith, through such a personal and living acquaintance with truth as changes the articles of our creed into the felt realities of existence.

The reader will have perceived that the thoughts on Revelation with which his attention has now been engaged, have all direct reference to the three conditions of mind noticed at the outset, as marking severally three classes of men, in whom any supposed assault on Revelation will, in the first instance at least, produce increased confidence in the rightness of their own position in relation to truth, namely: 1. Those whose faith in Revelation rests on the assumed authority of the Church. 2. Those who have ceased to believe in Revelation. 3. Those who have a true faith in Revelation, living in the light of the truth it reveals. I have expressed the hope that, while the ordeal through which we are now passing may at the first have awakened in these three classes alike one and the same feeling, of which the expression in words would be, "We are right"; yet that, eventually, the discussions raised will not only deepen and strengthen true and living faith, but also effectually disturb in many the false peace of blind faith and of unbelief: while many in whom true and living faith is alloyed with superstition and unbelief, will have their faith purged from these, and be forced to take, consciously and avowedly, their true and proper standing as children of the light; —forced to fall back on their faith in the living God: a necessity which recals the words of Henry Dorney, "It is a profitable sweet necessity to be forced on the naked arm of Jehovah."

The ideal of Christianity will always transcend Christianity as actually realized in our experience: nevertheless, to judge our own Christianity aright, we must take it to the light of that ideal. No doubt, if this is done in a legal spirit, the result may be hurtful, and full of discouragement. If the divine ideal for us is at all contemplated as a requirement, it immediately becomes to us a "law working wrath." But in the true apprehension of the free grace of God it is quite otherwise. The divine ideal is then seen as the divine purpose and gift in Christ, that which God is bestowing—not demanding; the good to be received—not to be self-produced as a claim for acceptance; the heavenly treasure with which the earthen vessel of our humanity is to be filled—not a treasure to spring out of its emptiness. Understanding that salvation is " of grace, not of works," we can hear a gospel in such words as these: " Let the same mind be in you which was also in Christ Jesus." " Be ye therefore perfect even as your Father which is in heaven is perfect." When it is said, " Beloved, if our heart condemn us not, then have we confidence toward God," this is not to be understood as implying the conscious attainment of the ideal set before us, but only the conscious acceptance of that ideal, and that the divine choice for us has become our choice for ourselves: for with the unfeigned yielding of ourselves up to God, that He may fulfil in us the good pleasure of His goodness, there comes " the heart not condemning," and " confidence towards God."

Therefore the fullest recognition of what has now been urged as one aspect of Christianity, to wit, that it is a seeing light in God's light, can, if rightly understood, have no other result than to exalt our conception of the grace of God to man. Thus to raise our conception of that grace may be to humble us because we come so much short of our high calling; but we shall not the less thank God that our calling is so high. "Brethren, I count not myself to have apprehended; but this one thing I do, forgetting those things which are behind and reaching forth to those things which are before, I press toward the mark for the prize of the high calling of God in Christ Jesus."[1] If we see our Christian calling in the light of these words, we shall feel that the highest conception of it to which we attain may be kept before the mind without the risk of discouraging the feeblest faith, or of marring the comfort and peace which accompany the faintest dawn of divine light.

[1] Phil. iii. 13, 14.

PART II.

PART II.

I BELIEVE that those are now speaking the word that is most in season, who urge the Church to remember that light from its very nature must be its own witness, and that this must hold true in the highest sense of that which is in the highest sense light. I trust that what is here written to this effect may be received with that self-application without which it cannot profit. "Am I a child of the light and of the day? Am I seeing light in God's light?"—this is the personal question which I have desired to suggest. I have not prepared the way by first considering the elements of the provision which God has made for our participation in divine light. To attempt this would be to enter on a very wide field. The witness for God in creation and providence, and in the being and constitution of man; the teaching of history seen in its relation to God—especially of that history which has been distinguished by divine self-manifestation, demanding faith in the supernatural, and which we read by the light of an inspired comment; the self-evidencing glory of God in divine truth, together with the help for faith in the divine purpose for man, which even the partial fulfilment of that purpose in the Church affords; finally, that without which all this light from without would avail us nothing, namely, the dealing of the Holy Spirit with our individual spirits;—these all are elements in the divine provision for faith. But it was not necessary to my purpose to prepare the way by illustrating these, because they may be fully recognized, and yet the need for pressing the personal question, whether our faith is a conscious dwelling in the light of truth, may remain. Yet any teaching on the subject of Revelation, which does not embrace a direct consideration of the subject of Inspiration, must at this moment be disappointing. I shall now therefore endeavour briefly to express the thoughts on Inspiration which satisfy my own mind, and which I hope may commend themselves to others.

According to the faith of the Church from the beginning, the gift of divine light which we possess in the Bible is ascribed to Inspiration of the Holy Spirit; while all spiritual apprehension of divine light and all power to walk in it, is also referred to the same Holy Spirit. I shall, in order to keep the identity of source before the mind, speak of these two forms of Inspiration as, severally, the Inspiration of Revelation, and Inspiration of the Divine Life: while I shall consider them not only separately, but also with reference to each other.

This is the more needful, because while the Church recognises both these divers actings of the One Spirit, two opposite tendencies in regard to them are at present manifested, and demand special attention;—the tendency on the one hand to resolve the former into the latter, and to regard the Inspiration of Revelation as differing only in degree from that personal teaching of the Holy Spirit which we are all called to know; and the tendency on the other hand to leave the latter out of account in a trust in the former, as if Revelation were enough to make us partakers in the light of life, apart from the individual experience of the fulfilment of the promise, "They shall be all taught of God."

I.

A Divine Revelation is knowledge bestowed on us by God in the form of human thought and speech, the Holy Spirit employing men for this end. This is what we mean when we speak of the Scriptures as a Divine Revelation; while in a larger sense, all by which God utters Himself to us in creation and providence, and the divine constitution of things, is Revelation. But whether in the larger sense or in that which is more restricted, Revelation is really *Revelation* only as making something which God wills to communicate truly and perfectly known, *as far as respects the utterance of it.* To insist that a Revelation must express truly and perfectly what it is intended to convey, may seem superfluous; but readers who are familiar with the questions raised on this subject know that some, while acknowledging a peculiar and divine character to belong to the Scriptures, still hold that the nature of the human medium limits the extent to which divine light coming through it may be trusted. No doubt God's revelation of Himself through man, as also His revelation to man, is limited by what He Himself has made humanity to be; though when we think of humanity in the light of Christ the Son of God and the Son of Man, we may question how far we are justified in speaking of limits here at all. But it is one thing to say, that, because of human limits, what God can reveal of Himself to man is to be held to be less than what God is,—and it is quite another thing to say, that what God sees it good to reveal of Himself to man He cannot truly and effectually reveal through man,—that the medium must more or less colour and distort the light passing through it. This consistently held makes a revelation to man and a revelation through man equally impossible. If man cannot transmit light without distorting it, then neither can he receive light without misconceiving it.

The practical importance of this point is manifestly very great. If an inspired Apostle receives knowledge of a "mystery hid from ages and generations," and imparts that knowledge to us, conceiving truly and imparting truly, then it is only needful that we should be in the light of what he has written in order to be in the light of truth in that matter, so far as it has been God's purpose to reveal it. But if, after we know what the Apostle has written, and understand his words as he meant them to be understood, we have still to enquire how far it was possible for him to receive, and transmit truly, divine light,—how far his limits as a man, and besides these, his limits as an individual having a special mental history and education, have interfered with this, how can we call what is written a Divine Revelation at all?

I know that there are some who hesitate to receive the teaching of Prophets and Apostles as Revelation *in the sense now stated*, while still believing the Scriptures to contain higher and more important truth, and truth more to be traced to a divine source, than is to be found in any other writings: which truth they also study, setting themselves to separate it from the human element of error, the presence of which they assume. Certainly no problem as to disturbing forces could be more hopeless of solution than that seems to be, which on this system would meet us here at the threshold. But the conception of a Divine Revelation precludes such a problem. As we believe that God, who teaches us knowledge of Himself by the works of His hands, teaches us also by holy Apostles and Prophets a higher knowledge than these His material works can convey, so we also believe that in communicating that higher knowledge He presents it to us pure and unmixed, as in the case of the lower knowledge He confessedly does. It is not doubted that a true and infallible testimony for God is borne by the heavens and the earth,—a testimony which if we can hear it will not deceive us. We believe it is so also when an inspired Apostle declares the Gospel of the grace of God.

II.

But we believe that all Revelation, not only the Scriptures but also all else by which God speaks to us from without, is subordinate to the dealing of the Spirit of God with us in the inner man. This is the Inspiration of the Divine Life. It belongs to the dealing of God with our individual spirits in that kingdom of God which is within us, and is affected, as to its course and manifestation in our consciousness, by the measure of response on our part—the yielding of our spirits to the divine Spirit.

The Inspiration of the Divine Life being personal to us individually, all that regards it might be expected to be well understood by us, however the case might be as to that Inspiration of Revelation of which we have no experience. Yet this is not so; no, not even to the extent of the distinct recognition of the fact of such Inspiration. The light shines in the darkness, but the darkness comprehends it not. Our liberty to hear or not to hear becomes in effect the possibility of not even knowing that we are spoken to. Sometimes when the divine voice is heard and recognised, the feeling of him that hears will express itself in the words of Jacob, "Surely the Lord is in this place, and I knew it not."[1] But this is not always felt: on the contrary, it is apt to be assumed that God has spoken only when men have heard. Nay, it is a remarkable fact, that of those who most fully recognize all true reception of divine light, all true faith, as of the operation of the Holy Spirit, a considerable number limit His operation

[1] Gen. xxviii. 16.

to those who manifest this true faith; making the result in man the measure of the divine acting;—while yet they hold, however inconsistently, that all men are responsible for that faith, which without such divine acting they believe to be impossible. But we are not taught to recognise an obligation to believe more wide than the presence of the power to believe. Our need of the Spirit and the gift of the Spirit are commensurate. The parental instinct, because of which if a son ask bread from any of us that is a father he will not give him a stone, is the universal revelation of this universal law; a fact in the natural world revealing a corresponding fact in the spiritual world. "If ye then being evil, know how to give good gifts unto your children: how much more shall your heavenly Father give the Holy Spirit to them that ask Him?"[1] We cannot understand these words of our Lord otherwise than as teaching that bestowing the Holy Spirit pertains to the divine Fatherliness as what is proper to it, and is therefore as universal as it is; being as essential to the life in respect of which we are God's offspring, as the food which parental care provides

[1] St. Luke xi. 14.

is to the life which we derive from our earthly parents. We must recognise the authority of this divine Revelation presented to us in the constitution of humanity. Indeed, unbelief here would be doubly condemned, seeing that, along with the light which is in the parental instinct itself, we have our Lord's comment on it and seal to it.

We believe that our heavenly Father freely bestows on us as His offspring the Inspiration of the Divine Life. But we do not conceive of the presence of the Holy Spirit with us, as of that of the air we breathe or the light of day, and neither do we conceive of His acting, as we conceive of physical laws of which we may or may not avail ourselves at our own choice, and in a way that implies no manifestation of a personal will besides our own. *That* is the case as to all the power which we enjoy through knowledge of mere laws, as that of the expansion of steam, for example. But *here* another will besides our will is recognised by us—a present giving on the part of God, who shapes His dealing with us to our dealing with Him, while with one unchanging purpose of love. At one time we trace the divine observance of the law that "unto him that hath shall be given, and from him that hath not shall be taken away what he seemeth to have;" and, spiritually, the words are fulfilled, "the hand of the diligent maketh rich, and slothfulness covereth a man with rags:" and then again we see that the circle of the operation of this law *lies within a wider circle* in which the "mercy which endureth for ever" rules, and those receive anew, who have forfeited by misuse, that which had been given to them, and as it were a fresh start is graciously granted to them, and even past loss is turned to gain: and so *through the grace of God* it becomes true—

"That men may rise on stepping-stones
Of their dead selves to higher things."

"Whatsoever a man soweth that shall he also reap;"[1] yet—"if Thou, Lord, shouldest mark iniquities, O Lord, who shall stand? But there is forgiveness with Thee that Thou mayest be feared."[2] "O Israel, thou hast destroyed thyself, but in me is thine help found."[3] In that kingdom of God which is within us, there are divine actings which correspond with that which God did outwardly, when the Apostles of the risen Saviour were sent forth to preach the

[1] Gal. vi. 7.   [2] Ps. cxxx. 3, 4.   [3] Hosea xiii. 9.

Gospel, "beginning at Jerusalem;" and forgiveness of sins in Christ's blood was first proclaimed to the men who had crucified the Lord. A Personal Will, and not a mere spiritual law, demands our faith; and what we experience is now according to the words, "Draw nigh to God and He will draw nigh to you;"[1] and now to the words, "I am found of them that sought me not."[2] In that lower region of social existence in which the persons are men with men, we meet what is analogous to this. A willing pupil makes a willing teacher, and happy progress: but the unwilling pupil is not left unchecked to take his own way; otherwise the idleness of to-day would cause that there should be no lesson on the morrow. So, realising personality in the acting of the Holy Spirit, we see how much there may be of diversity in His dealings with individual spirits, and that we cannot trace them all to one simple law, but must refer them to the exercise of a merciful judgment on the part of all-wise and all-enduring love. Thus when a reckless profligate is suddenly arrested in his sinful course, by some ray of divine light coming to him with subduing

[1] James iv. 8.   [2] Isaiah lxv. 1.

power—it may be a text of Scripture, learned in childhood, but long dormant within him, or some counsel of parental love hitherto despised—we cannot say that now he is reaping what he had sown, or that the new life which henceforth he may live is related as effect to cause to what he had hitherto been. What we are contemplating is not the operation of a law of which the man has wisely availed himself. It is divine grace—the act of the Holy Spirit.

Cases like this not wisely considered have led to speculations confining within limits, more or less narrow, the dealing of the Holy Spirit with the spirits of men, and to the discussion of such questions as,—whether divine grace may be resisted or is to be assumed to have been present only when it has prevailed, or whether it is sometimes what may be resisted and sometimes irresistible. But though we cannot wonder that in the deep sense of God's part in what takes place, and while finding nothing in himself to have led to it or to have given a claim for it, the man who is the subject of strongly marked grace may call it irresistible and sovereign, and in his self-abasement and self-abjuration may use language which seems to be putting his seal to the narrowest creed, there is no warrant for saying that even in such a case grace has been irresistible, or that it has been the manifestation of a mere arbitrary will, and not of a will to save, which, in manifesting itself in so marked a way, is preaching a Gospel to every sinner. "Howbeit, for this cause I obtained mercy, that in me first Jesus Christ might shew forth all long-suffering, for a pattern to them which should hereafter believe on Him to life everlasting."[1] When the divine Wisdom says, "I love them that love me, and those that seek me early shall find me," the Gospel is preached to us; but the deep fountain of love from which that Gospel flows is still more revealed, when God makes Himself known to one who has sinned with a high hand, it may be through youth and manhood, and the aged sinner is seen receiving the kingdom of God as a little child.

But it is not only in these more strongly marked instances of mercy rejoicing against judgment, that the great distinction between having to do with a law and having to do with the living God, is illustrated by our spiritual

[1] 1 Tim. i. 16.

experience. No one can be without illustration of this distinction in his own case, who considers what the pure and unmixed action of the law "Whatsoever a man soweth that shall he also reap" would have made his own history. Of the operation of that law we all have had abundant experience, both outwardly and inwardly. But neither outwardly nor inwardly has its course been supreme: for outwardly, the providence of God in the ordering of our circumstances has crossed our wayward path with monitions for good, using both persons and things for this end, while we have not sought good; and inwardly, the same forgiving persevering love of our Heavenly Father has been manifested in the striving of the Holy Spirit with us,—it may be at the time felt as such,—it may be afterwards in the retrospect confessed with "sad relentings," though at the time blindly resisted. No one seeking the kingdom of God as his first and great interest, and knowing that kingdom as it is revealing itself within him, can be ignorant that not the mere observance or neglect of a law on his own part has determined the course of things there—however clear the operation of law there has been—but that a Living Will, watchful and wise, has been suiting the manifestation of its love to his changing states.

III.

This experience of a Personal God in the Inspiration of the Divine Life, so broadly distinguished from our experience of mere laws, must help our faith in Revelation, because it is an experience in that region above law, to which Revelation belongs. Yet we suppose a manner of manifestation of the Divine Personality, and a consciousness of personal intercourse with God, in the case of those who are honoured to be the channels of Divine Revelation, differing from our experience, and which apart from experience we cannot expect to understand. Our experience is of light coming to us from without becoming spiritual light to us, and awakening a response within us. This is so whether what thus comes to us with living power has been now presented to us for the first time, or has been, it may be, long familiar to us and accepted by us as a form of thought, or a revealed fact full of spiritual power being spiritually apprehended, but which, while not so apprehended, could be held in the memory with profitless acknowledgment. But with whatever intelligent consciousness we refer to the Holy Spirit the transition in ourselves from a mere traditional historical faith of what God has revealed to a living faith in which we see light in God's light, we do not suppose that our experience enables us to know the nature of that consciousness of being receiving a communication from God, which we must assume when that which God makes known to a man is presented to him not from without, but immediately, and as direct from God. This we must suppose in the *original* impartation even of that which is essential light. But we know that a great deal of what God has imparted to individual men that they might make it known to others, has not been essential light—however related to it in the Divine counsels, and however instrumental in its own place in connection with man's spiritual education.

This applies to a very large proportion of what God spoke to Moses. It applies to the word of the Lord which came to the Prophets, not only in so far as that word was in our common sense of the term prophetic, that is, referring to a future more or less remote, but also in so far as it conferred a divine authority to go as messengers from God to kings and princes and peoples in their own time. This applies also to such individual cases as that of Abraham, to whom God spoke of the distant future,—though in relation to himself and in acknowledgment of his personal faith; from whom also was required trust in divine words which had not their light in themselves; as to which, we can understand how, being known to be certainly spoken by God Himself, it was a faith which gave glory to God—a faith to be accounted righteousness—in Abraham to trust in them against sight and sense; but which, from their very nature, it is manifest that Abraham could not refer to God because of any spiritual light which was in them. To us at this distance, and looking back through the ages, the history of Jew and Gentile justifies the faith of the Father of the faithful: but his own knowledge that it was God that spoke to him—that in believing he was believing God—must have been at once clear and certain, and a manner of knowledge of which we have no experience.

I am speaking, it will be observed, of the distinctive consciousness which may be assumed to have accompanied the distinctive Inspiration of Revelation,—not of what justifies us in believing in the fact of such Inspiration, which is altogether another matter: and what I say only amounts to this, that the nature of the function which we ascribe to those through whom that light which we receive in the study of the Scriptures under the teaching of the Holy Spirit was first given, implies this distinction between their experience and ours; so that we are prepared for the language which they use. But, apart from this, we cannot hesitate to receive their own account of the matter. The character of a true man whose truth has approved itself to us, justifies our faith in his statements as to matters beyond our experience, but known to him. The same principle, but with much surer operation, justifies our receiving implicitly from those through whom God has made important revelations, their own account of His imparting these to them.

The distinction between the Inspiration of Revelation and that divine teaching which enables us individually to apprehend spiritual truth, has always been recognised by the Church; and we are placed in a new position when it is called in question. We have long been familiar with controversies as to what the Bible teaches, among those who have been all agreed in admitting the authority of the Bible as inspired, and so have all appealed to it, however differently they have understood it. But it is quite recently that a certain reverence for the Bible and recognition of it as a source of light has been connected with denying to the sacred writers any other inspiration than that—whatever it is held to be—which is present in that spiritual insight in which we are all called to share. If the distinction we have been accustomed to make is real, it cannot be rejected without loss: and in favour of the belief that it is real, there is not only that testimony of the sacred writers themselves which ought here to be conclusive, but there is the fact that so much of what is communicated as by divine authority, is what no peculiar degree of spiritual insight could enable men to know. As has been noticed already, much of what we learn from the sacred record, is not of a spiritual nature at all; but even when that which is written is in its highest aspect purely spiritual, and what is only truly known when spiritually discerned, the spiritual is presented to us in divine facts, which *as facts* could only become known by Revelation. The divine facts are commended to our faith by the glory of God which shines in them, and by the light which they shed on our condition as subjects of the kingdom of God; but as facts they could never have become the subjects of human knowledge, excepting by such inspiration as we ascribe to holy Apostles and Prophets. The great facts which our faith embraces are as the links of a divine chain, of which some links have had a visibility here on earth, while the rest belong entirely to the invisible. But even of those links which have been visible—the life and death of the Son of God—the whole *spiritual* aspect has been invisible, and could only be known to man by Revelation. The life of Christ as the light of men, the death of Christ as the sacrifice for sin, could no more be known apart from Inspiration, than the Incarnation or the Resurrection of Christ from the dead, or His presence at the right hand of the Father, or His having all power in heaven and on earth, or His being the judge of quick and dead. But if we believe these to be facts—the great realities of existence to us, in the light of which alone God and man are truly known—we must receive the Inspiration by which alone they could be known, as another fact belonging to the same high region of the grace of God to man.

There are other departments of knowledge in which the knowledge, being once attained, is held with a certainty which springs out of the knowledge itself, and is in no respect confidence in the channel through which we have received it. This is true of mathematical knowledge for example. A mathematical capacity enables a man to hold the truth of the highest discoveries in that region with as much confidence as the discoverer, and with a confidence equally independent. But here this confidence in the light is accompanied by the conviction that the discoverer has differed from the man who is taught by him only in degree of mathematical capacity. What enables him to understand he knows might, carried to a higher power, have enabled him to discover. It is quite otherwise, however, when, in the exercise of a spiritual capacity, we understand the mystery hid from ages and generations, and made known to the Apostles, and by them communicated to us. The capacity of apprehending and adoring, we know, is common to them, and to us, and to the millions who have believed through their word. It is even possible that among these millions, many have had a greater measure of that capacity developed in them by the Holy Spirit, than these Apostles themselves. But what we feel distinguishes them from all these millions, as well as from ourselves, is, that this mystery was revealed to them, and has been made known to us only through them.

The facts of Christianity imply by their very nature the Inspiration of Revelation in those through whom they have been made known; and this is our answer to any who profess any recognition of these facts, and yet deny that Inspiration: and I believe that this answer is not only that which presents itself when we are forced to think, being pressed for a reason of our faith, but is also the reason which without thinking has weighed with us, and lies at the foundation of our faith in Inspiration. Should we have all believed in Inspiration, had the Bible revealed nothing which did not on its very face appear to be what could not have been known without Inspiration? But the great facts which our faith has been embracing being all what it has been felt could not have been otherwise known, our faith in Inspiration has been inseparable from our faith in them. And in truth, *the real ultimate interest of the question of Inspiration is the high and paramount interest of the great facts our knowledge of which we owe to Inspiration.* No doubt, these facts being known and spiritually apprehended, the light of the glory of God in them is their great and absolute hold on our faith. But the reflex effect of this as to Inspiration is not only to establish and confirm our faith in its reality, but also to convince us of its absolute necessity, seeing that while the spiritual discernment granted to us enables us to recognise the word of God in the lips of the Apostles, " receiving it not as the word of men but as it is in truth the word of God,"[1] we could not by any measure of the same capacity have anticipated that word of ourselves. " How shall they believe in Him of whom they have not heard? and how shall they hear without a preacher?"[2]

We recognise then two distinct Inspirations: first, the Inspiration to which we owe Revelation, bestowed on some for the good of all; and

---

[1] 1 Thess. ii. 13.   [2] Rom. x. 14.

second, the operation of the Divine Spirit in individual spirits, enabling us to receive and walk in the light of the Revelation thus given, as well as in all divine light however bestowed. And the distinctness in this diversity of operation of the One Spirit is such, that those who are honoured to be the subjects of the former Inspiration as Prophets or Apostles, yet need as men to partake of the latter, and only in the measure in which they do so, have themselves the spiritual benefit of the Revelation of which they are the channels. Doubtless those to whom the word of God comes may be supposed to be already men of God in regard to the spirit of their own minds—although there is at least one marked exception recorded—but the distinction here is not the less real. The Apostle, to whom the mystery hid from ages and generations was revealed, that through him it might be made known to all, needed as much as those to whom he proclaimed that mystery as glad tidings, to live in the Spirit and walk in the Spirit, that the light of the Revelation made through him might be to himself the light of life. His prayer for the Ephesians was doubtless equally his prayer for himself. "For this cause I bow my knees unto the Father of our Lord Jesus Christ, of whom the whole family in heaven and earth is named, that He would grant you, according to the riches of his glory, to be strengthened with might by His Spirit in the inner man; that Christ may dwell in your hearts by faith; that ye, being rooted and grounded in love, may be able to comprehend with all saints what is the breadth and length and depth and height, and to know the love of Christ, which passeth knowledge, that ye might be filled with all the fulness of God."[1] That God was "able to do exceeding abundantly above all that they could ask or think according to the power that worked in them," (ver. 20) was the measure of his hope for them and for himself. But his experience in at first receiving immediately from God the light which he had imparted to them—this they were not to share. There was no reason why they should. In the membership that is in Christ they were in this matter debtors to him. The distinction now insisted on we best study as it is presented to us in the case of the Apostles, in whom Revelation culminated, and in whom it closed, and in whom also the Divine Life was

[1] Ephes. iii. 14—19.

present in the richest form of the rich first-fruits of the Gospel. And the instruction we thus receive is made very clear by the circumstance that St. Paul is led to contrast the Inspiration of Revelation with that of the Divine Life,—not as here in order to demand faith for the former, for as to this there was then no question,—but to teach the Church their relative importance. "Though I have the gift of prophecy, and understand all mysteries and all knowledge, and have not charity, I am nothing."[1]

To those who do not recognise the distinctive Inspiration of Revelation, the Inspiration of the Scriptures is but the reflected Inspiration of the Church. According to this view the Scriptures do not shine with an immediate divine light. They only give back what of the teaching of God had taken effect in the Church of each successive generation. We only learn from them, therefore, what the Church understood,—not what God meant the Church to understand. But it was not the light of their time that the prophets gave forth. It was light that condemned their time, and with divine authority. It was light which separated from their generation those to whom it

[1] 1 Cor. xiii. 2.

came, and on whom the burden of making it known was laid; placing them on one side with God, and their generation,—the Church of their time,—on the other. The series of the Inspired stands out from all the generations to which they individually belonged, one series by reason of the one light which shines from them all, and which by its unity vindicates for itself one source. We do not regard these men as but the better specimens of their several generations, more influenced than the rest by a divine teaching common to all. Such they may have been, but they were manifestly more and other than this, and apart from the recognition of them by our Lord, we feel that in proportion as we come to know divine light, they are to us lights shining in darkness condemning the darkness, rejected also by the darkness. Accordingly, this is the relation of the Church of each time to the succession of Prophets in the retrospect of the first martyr. "Ye stiff-necked and uncircumcised in heart and ears, ye do always resist the Holy Ghost: as your fathers did, so do ye. Which of the prophets have not your fathers persecuted? and they have slain them which shewed before of the coming of the Just One; of whom ye have been now the betrayers and murderers. Who have received the law by the disposition of angels, and have not kept it."¹ That these prophets expressed not the light of their time, but that the light of all time—the eternal light—expressed itself through them, is the conviction received by us, not only from their position of antagonism to their time, but from this other fact also, that the light in what they spoke, was beyond what they themselves understood; "Of which salvation the prophets have enquired and searched diligently, who prophesied of the grace that should come unto you: searching what, or what manner of time the Spirit of Christ, which was in them, did signify, when it testified beforehand the sufferings of Christ, and the glory that should follow. Unto whom it was revealed, that not unto themselves, but unto us they did minister the things which are now reported unto you by them that have preached the gospel unto you with the Holy Ghost sent down from heaven; which things the angels desire to look into."²

If the writings of the Prophets have not the high character now claimed for them, how should they have any interest for us beyond—what

¹ Acts vii. 51—53.   ² 1 Peter i. 10—12.

would doubtless still be great—a pure historic interest? but as teachers, how should they have an *abiding* interest, seeing that we belong to a dispensation so in advance of theirs, and a dispensation which is distinctively that of the Spirit? When we consider the time and circumstances of Timothy,—his relation to the great Apostle of the Gentiles, whose own son he was in the faith, —the abundance of spiritual gifts then in the Church,—the gift in Timothy himself personally,— we must see that the place given to the Scriptures in the Apostle's exhortation to him is most instructive: "And that from a child thou hast known the Holy Scriptures which are able to make thee wise unto salvation through faith which is in Christ Jesus."[1] These Scriptures were, we know, the Old Testament Scriptures. How did they retain their value in the full blaze of Gospel light, in the first outpouring of the promised Comforter, the Spirit of truth, who was to guide unto all truth? How were they not now out of date, or how at all could they, if but a reflection from the Church of former ages, make Timothy "wise unto salvation through faith which is in Christ Jesus?" Their retaining such a place as the

[1] 2 Tim. iii. 13.

Apostle here gives them, is inexplicable on any view of their character, but that which the Apostle himself immediately adds, "All Scripture is given by inspiration of God, and is profitable for doctrine, for reproof, for correction, for instruction in righteousness; that the man of God may be perfect, throughly furnished unto all good works."

"It is written in the Prophets, And they shall be all taught of God. Every man, therefore, that hath heard and hath learned of the Father cometh unto me."[1] No doubt the personal teaching of God, which we are all called to know, is that to which we are ultimately brought, as that to which alone the true consciousness of light belongs. Our faith must stand in the power of God. No outward Revelation can enlighten us spiritually while we resist the Divine Spirit within us. While so resisting, no beauty of the lily, no glory of the sun in the firmament, no return of seed-time and harvest, nor gift of rain from heaven, and fruitful seasons, will work faith in us. "The rebellious dwell in a dry land," and "shall not know when good cometh." And as to the Scriptures, whatever

[1] St. John vi. 45.

the true conception of their nature be, they cannot yield their treasures to us so long as we are the wise and prudent who lean to their own understanding; while, were they only what the view now rejected would make them, namely, the best and most spiritual experiences, and greatest measures of spiritual light of the best men of the generations from which they have come down to us, they would still have a value, and the truly teachable would welcome what of light is in them. This is true. But if we understand how inward divine teaching is related to what comes to us from without, the former enabling us to receive the latter but not superseding it, we must value as above all price, and to be defended with a holy jealousy, the gift of divine Revelation—pure light from the first while progressing in fulness; and however varied in its form, and whatever of mere human history it takes up, leaving to him who reverently sets himself to hear the Word of God, no room for uncertainty as to what comes to him with divine authority "for doctrine, for reproof, for correction, for instruction in righteousness."

And here it is important to notice, as there seems to be sometimes a confusion of thought in regard to it, that the question of the Canon of Scripture, and the question of the Inspiration of Scripture, are in no way to be confounded. The Old Testament Canon we receive now, as it was recognised by the Old Testament Church. The New Testament Canon, the New Testament Church, after a time felt called to fix, and proceeded to ascertain and fix accordingly. We believe that this was done in a simplicity of purpose, and with a diligent care and with the possession of advantages for judging on the part of those who were in God's providence called to the solemn task which justifies confidence; and we believe the result has been such as to indicate a divine ordering. But the question of Inspiration is altogether prior to, and independent of this matter. The existence of inspired writings having divine authority, was a fact known and familiar to the Church from the beginning. The New Testament Scriptures, successively, as they were written, added themselves to the Old in the Canon of men's faith, as new stars appearing in the firmament would take their place among the stars of heaven. How could men hesitate to receive as Holy Scripture the Epistle of an Apostle who had preached the Gospel with the Holy

Ghost sent down from heaven, "the Lord working with him and confirming the word with signs following?"[1] Because of the circumstances of the Church these additions to Scripture were not, so to speak, visible to all in all places at the same moment. Some in one place received one Epistle; others elsewhere, another. In process of time these treasures, scattered among the several Churches, became known to the Church generally, and were recognised as a part of their common wealth. The fulness of living light,— the presence in the Church of so many who had heard many times from the Apostles' own lips that which their Epistles contained, and doubtless more fully, and with varied illustration and expansion—as when "Paul preached unto them, ready to depart on the morrow," and continued his speech until midnight," and afterwards "talked a long while, even till break of day,"— caused any need of ascertaining a Canon not to be felt for a time. The circumstances of the world and of the Church would also have made the attempt difficult, even were more call for it felt; so the delay in the formal proposal to ascertain a Canon is sufficiently explained: but whether

[1] St. Mark xvi. 20.

or not the attempt was made at the best time, or whether the Canon, when fixed, included some writings rashly, or excluded others that ought to have received a place, is a question totally distinct from that of Inspiration. We have every reason, so far as we can judge, to be thankful for the care and discrimination with which the task attempted appears to have been accomplished. That so little criticism has been offered—so little of what was received ever been called in question —is surely a favourable testimony of much weight. But we must never forget, though some seem in danger of forgetting it, that fixing the Canon was not stamping a divine authority on anything. It was only the recognition of the fact, that certain writings were already held to be divine, and had separated themselves from all else that was held of estimation by the Church, as being what remained to them of the teaching of the divinely-inspired founders of the Church. Our faith in the Bible in no respect turns upon any supposed infallible guidance enjoyed by the framers of the Canon. None of the great men, Luther, Calvin, or the rest whose names have been quoted, as one doubting the claim to a place in the Canon of one portion of Scripture, and another of another, ever felt these historical doubts in the least affecting their faith or the value of the Bible to them. How could they? It filled them, and held them, and ruled them, by its own divine light, as it should us.

The Inspiration of Revelation has peculiar difficulty for persons in that state of mind in which science and philosophy are still conceived to be opposed to the recognition of any Inspiration which amounts to a personal dealing of the Divine Spirit with our spirits. Some kind of presence of a divine light of spiritual truth with the human mind such persons feel able to acknowledge, though they would rather call it "the pure reason" than Inspiration; and to the conscious knowledge of this light they can believe that in all ages some may have attained beyond others, and also, that as the ages have advanced there has been a progress in the measure of the light thus attained: and so "the Inspiration of the Bible" is an expression which they can use with a philosophic meaning, that is to say, they can ascribe to the inspired writers a greater measure of profiting by this universal light, in consequence of which they became severally the most enlightened men of their times. But this is all. The difficulties which men of this cast of mind must encounter in their study of the Bible, are very obvious. Pure principles,—all commending of righteousness whether in the Old Testament or the New—whether the Ten Commandments or the Sermon on the Mount,—they can of course accept: but all that represents God as manifesting Himself personally—the great facts of our Redemption—must present to them insuperable difficulties, if the Bible record in all its details be allowed to remain unquestioned. What measure of liberty will be taken with that record, will depend on the measure of freedom from the restraint of ordinary habits of religious thought and feeling which has been reached, and the extent to which the theory of Inspiration, assumed and set out with, is made the test of what is to be received. There is therefore a risk of being felt to do injustice in the case of those who have advanced but a small way in this path, if we argue from the extreme case—though that doubtless best illustrates a tendency. We know also that elements of divine truth may be present with saving power, even where there is the taint of error. But whatever be the true estimate of any individual case, we know that there is a process of thought on this subject, which in its extreme development amounts to nothing short of eliminating from Christianity its great facts; while yet it is proposed to retain and acknowledge that spiritual essence of eternal truth to which we know that we have reached only through the faith of these facts, and which we believe that we could not have otherwise attained. I refer to that way of dealing with Christianity, in which the ideal for man which Christianity has revealed is professedly accepted, and the faith that God is love is also accepted, and the relation of these to each other is recognised—that because God is love He wills that we should be like Him, dwelling in love and so dwelling in Him;—while yet that work of God in Christ which reveals the love that is in God, and that divine constitution of humanity in Christ which provides for the fulfilment in us of the desire and purpose of that love, are rejected. *The divine fruit is professedly acknowledged, while we are asked to regard as a myth the divine tree—the True Vine— which bears it!* The belief that by some process of accretion, a nucleus of ethical teaching could gather to itself a mythical history, such as the

Scriptures are assumed to contain, presents itself, surely, as the strange and incredible inversion of that divine order according to which the faith of the facts of Revelation, working by the love which they reveal, raises us to the light of the eternal life. A state of mind like this, in which the facts of religion are regarded as difficulties to be explained—difficulties so great, as to gain acceptance for any theory, however extravagant, which offers to explain them away—is the very opposite of that of the Apostles, who connect continually their highest apprehensions of truth with these facts, as being to them the very Revelation of that truth. No consciousness of being in light which has in itself the witness of light, can be more unmistakeable than that of the Apostle John in speaking of love as that which God is, and in which God wills man to dwell. But how came he to this light? "In this was manifested the love of God toward us, because that God sent His only-begotten Son into the world, that we might live through Him. Herein is love, not that we loved God, but that He loved us, and sent His Son to be the propitiation for our sins."[1] So St. Paul, exhorting

[1] 1 John iv. 9, 10.

the Philippians to "work out their own salvation with fear and trembling" in the faith that "God worked in them to will and to do of His good pleasure,"[1] teaches them to see their salvation—the divine idea for man, to be wrought in them by God Himself—in the mind that was in Christ Jesus (ver. 5), and illustrates that mind of Christ and the divine authority with which it claimed their faith, by the history of the work of the Son as our Saviour, and the Father's acceptance of it. "Who, being in the form of God, thought it not robbery to be equal with God; but made Himself of no reputation, and took upon Him the form of a servant, and was made in the likeness of men: and being found in fashion as a man, He humbled Himself and became obedient unto death, even the death of the cross. Wherefore God also hath highly exalted Him, and given Him a name which is above every name: that at the name of Jesus every knee should bow, of things in heaven, and things in earth, and things under the earth; and that every tongue should confess that Jesus Christ is Lord, to the glory of God the Father." We are in no uncertainty in the case of the Apostles

[1] Phil. ii. 12, 13.

as to the relation in which the divine life they were living stood to the divine facts they were believing; and our confidence in the truthfulness of their testimony, both as to what they knew personally, and as to what was communicated to them by the Inspiration of Revelation, places us, according to the measure of our faith, in their position, rendering the facts which we know through them realities to us also, and bringing us under their power: "for we are built upon the foundation of the Apostles and Prophets, Jesus Christ Himself being the chief corner-stone."[1]

This therefore is the place and value of Revelation: it makes the light imparted by Inspiration to Prophets and Apostles, ours, as truly as it would be if the Inspiration had been granted to ourselves. No one not realising this can realise what that treasure is of which those would deprive us who could shake our faith in Revelation. As to those who attempt to do so, there is always a temptation to see others in such cases from our own stand-point, not from theirs: and so men to whom Inspiration is an open question, and who without the feeling of having much staked on the issue, are occupied in weighing

[1] Eph. ii. 20.

the subject critically, and men who have never doubted, and who have through what they have believed been living what they know to be eternal life, do not easily bear with one another; and the former are ready to charge the latter with illiberality, and the latter to charge the former with insidious designs. In such mutual recrimination neither party carries the conscience of the other along with them, and therefore neither can really help or benefit the other; yet faith should be calm and temperate—and so it will be in proportion as it is living faith; and so also should philosophy be calm and temperate—and true philosophy will be so. But, alas! even believing men do not always abide in Christ; and the purest search for truth does not always save men from that impatience with injustice done to our motives, which belongs to wounded self-love.

IV.

I now pass from Revelation and unbelief in respect to the Inspiration which Revelation implies, to speak of what seems to me at this moment to call for our attention not less loudly:

I mean that dealing of the Holy Spirit with our individual spirits, of which I have spoken as the Inspiration of the Divine Life, and the unbelief which exists as to it—for such unbelief does exist, and is widely spread, though more in a practical than distinctly doctrinal form.

In distinguishing the Inspiration of Revelation as it existed in the Apostles from that working of the Holy Spirit in them by which they lived the Divine Life, and which was common to them and to those they taught, we saw that the subordination of the former to the latter was clearly recognised by the great Apostle of the Gentiles; and that he who excelled in gifts and in abundance of revelations, placed charity above these, holding them as nothing without charity; while charity without them was still eternal life. Thus of the two divine workings present in Apostles, of which one has ceased while the other remains, we see that that which remains was held to be the greater while they still existed together, and this in the estimation of the men who knew both in the clear light of their own conscious experience; and they enable us to see that this estimate was just, teaching us that the *highest* knowledge of

God—that which is true and absolute—belongs not to the distinctive Inspiration of Revelation, but to the Divine Life. "Love is of God, and every one that loveth is born of God and knoweth God. He that loveth not knoweth not God; for God is love."[1] The important light which is thus shed on our own high calling in Christ and our place in the kingdom of God, shews the Apostles to us as a double gift; so that however high the preeminence which belongs to them as those through whom the knowledge of the gospel of our salvation has come to us, our debt to them and their interest to us are not less regarding them as men who sealed the truth they taught by what they were, and demonstrated in themselves our nearness to God in Christ. "I am crucified with Christ: nevertheless I live; yet not I, but Christ liveth in me: and the life which I now live in the flesh I live by the faith of the Son of God, who loved me, and gave himself for me."[2] "The Son of God is come, and hath given us an understanding, that we may know him that is true, and we are in him that is true, even in his Son Jesus Christ. This is the true God and eternal life."[3]

But though what the Apostles were as Christ-

---

[1] 1 John iv. 7, 8.   [2] Gal. ii. 20.   [3] 1 John v. 20.

ian men sealed the truth which as Apostles they were honoured to preach, and though they were thus a *double gift* to the Church, they are too often regarded more as teaching what we are to believe, than as shewing in themselves what we are called to be; and that Inspiration of Revelation which belonged to them as laying the foundations of the Church, more engages our attention than that Inspiration of the Divine Life which we and the whole Church are called to share with them. The evil that thus arises is very great, and it is also widespread. We have at this present time our attention specially drawn to the Inspiration of Revelation; and I have now offered to the reader's attention some of the thoughts on this subject which recent discussions have suggested, as what all readers of the Bible are competent to weigh for themselves, and as having the commendation that they make no demand for much research or critical investigation; being such that we cannot be asked to keep our judgment of their force suspended on the result of any such investigation. That there are true grounds for faith which may be thus judged of without waiting the issue of historical criticism, is clearly implied in the existence of any responsibility for faith in the mass of mankind. This is certain, whether the reasons now offered be among these grounds of faith or not. But, if the knowledge and understanding of the Sacred Writings within the reach of all, is such as justifies faith in the Inspiration of Revelation, irrespective of historical criticism—whatever interest or value such criticism has in its own place,—still more must the Bible place those who know it, and are guided by it in the path of life, in a condition to hold with the most entire assurance that other Inspiration which belongs to the Divine Life; as to which in truth our calling is not to be *believers* only, but *witnesses*. Yet while this is so, and we might be expected to be specially jealous for the Inspiration which is our own—ours by the gift of God, as eternal life is ours—it is most certain that there is not the same readiness to plead for Christianity as the Inspiration of living men—an Inspiration now sustaining a Divine Life in men, and enabling them to say, "Hereby know we that we dwell in Him and He in us, because He hath given us of His Spirit"[1]—as there is to defend Christianity as having come to us from God through inspired

[1] 1 John iv. 13.

men. I know that what is regarded as the orthodox creed recognises both Inspirations: but it is not the less the case that many who regard the Inspiration of Revelation as a sacred thing, manifest no corresponding faith in the Inspiration of the Divine Life; although it is clear that the faith of the former should imply the faith of the latter, inasmuch as the Scriptures which are derived from the former continually testify of the latter. Our Lord said to the multitude of the believers in Revelation in His day, "Ye search the Scriptures; for in them ye think ye have eternal life: and they are they which testify of me. And ye will not come unto me that ye might have life."[1] May not these words be now to many the same rebuke in reference to the Holy Spirit which they were in reference to the Son of God? Surely our contending for the Inspiration of the holy men of old, who "spake as they were moved by the Holy Ghost," while we refuse for ourselves that Inspiration of the same Holy Spirit in which the love of our God calls us to share, is too like the case of those who built the sepulchres of the Prophets whom their fathers slew, and yet by their rejection of

[1] St. John v. 39, 40.

the Son of God identified themselves with the deeds of their fathers.

I have said above that personal experience of the Inspiration of the Divine Life, and acquaintance with God in the light of that kingdom of God which is within us, help our faith in the Inspiration of Revelation: and so also it appears to me that the faith that "holy men of old spake as they were moved by the Holy Ghost" helps the faith of that universal Inspiration of the Holy Spirit which we are individually called to partake in. This is so, not only because the fact of the gift of the Spirit is a part of revealed truth, but still more because this Dispensation of the Spirit is that higher and more perfect kingdom of God to which previous dispensations looked forward, as that in which we were to be "builded together for an habitation of God through the Spirit."[1] All that we call supernatural,—and I use the word as the expression of a real distinction, though some in jealousy for the due recognition of the presence of God in all things would avoid it,— all that is a subordinating of the lower kingdom of nature to the higher kingdom of grace which has caused difficulty to those who recognise no

[1] Eph. ii. 22.

higher light than that of science, has its *ultimate* explanation only in that personal nearness of men to God and living communion with the Father of their spirits, which in its full development belongs distinctively to Christianity. Yet—in painful contradiction to what is thus the distinctive character of our dispensation—the fact is, as I have said, that while the Inspiration of Revelation is jealously defended, the Inspiration of the Divine Life is too often, if not denied, practically made no account of.

One cause at least of this evil is the misuse of Revelation, which has become to many a substitute for, instead of being subordinate to, the Inspiration of the Divine Life. In the early Christian Church, as the Epistles make it known to us, we see a life of communion with the Father and the Son in the Spirit. In this life we see the record of the past dealings of God with men, as well as the great facts of the work of redemption, dwelling in men by faith, and known in the light of love, through that strengthening with might by the Spirit in the inner man sought in the prayer of the Apostle for the Ephesians. No experience of receiving light from the Scriptures,—no sense of obligation to Prophets or

Apostles, is seen to hinder or qualify men's consciousness of being children of the light and of the day; the Spirit bearing witness with their spirits that they were the children of God. At the same time Revelation is seen to receive the honour due to it as the original channel of the light dwelt in; and any questioning of its divine authority would clearly have been as unavailing to awaken doubts as the attempt to shake confidence in the trustworthiness of a guide sent to direct a man's steps to a happy home, after, led by that guide, he had reached that home—being now encompassed with all its home joys. This language may seem strong in speaking of any experience of men in this house of our pilgrimage; but the " earnest of the inheritance" as enjoyed in the Christian Church at the first, was manifestly quite enough to justify such a comparison: and let us bless God that that earnest of the inheritance in the experienced presence and enlightening of the promised Comforter, is to many now, and has been to many in all ages of the Church, such a seal as this to the Inspiration of Revelation. To believe otherwise would be to believe that our God had left Himself without living witnesses, and that the dispensation of the

Spirit—continued through the ages—has been without the fruit of living communion with the living God. Yet there can be no doubt that the amount of this experience in the Church has not accorded with the character of our dispensation, and that one hindrance has been the use of the gift of Revelation without reference to, and in practical neglect of, the promise of the Comforter, the Spirit of truth.

This great error has been possible only through not realising that gulf between the infallibility of Scripture and the consciousness of being ourselves individually in the light of truth, of which Romanism has made so much account—claiming to have bridged it over by the infallibility of the Church. The existence of this gulf not being realised, an infallible Bible, with our own intelligence to gather its teaching, has seemed enough for our need; and the teaching of the Holy Spirit not being felt necessary, the promise of that teaching has had no attraction. It is easy to see how in this way it has come to pass that the Bible has been honoured, and jealously guarded from the assaults of scepticism, while yet the personal teaching of the Holy Spirit who inspired the Bible has had no welcome—any more than if the

Bible had been intended to enable men to do without the living God, taking itself His place instead of leading to Him.

1. As there is little practical fruit of general complaints on such a subject as this, it seems necessary to notice some of the indications of practical unbelief in the Inspiration of the Divine Life, and of the consequent absence of the personal experience of peacefully dwelling in the light of truth. One such intimation forced on our attention at the present moment, is the tone which characterizes much of the excitement caused by the agitation of the question of the Inspiration of Revelation. A manner of instruction such as we possess in Revelation—so distinct from all the other means of knowledge which God has granted to men, and of which the distinction is the personal manifestation of God Himself as a living God—cannot be accepted by us with a true faith, without being regarded with deep religious reverence and gratitude. Calling it in question must therefore affect us as the attempt to take from us a divine gift of inestimable value. No personal experience of the teaching of the Holy Spirit—no independent certainty that belongs to

living faith—no proving in ourselves the truth of the words, "He that believeth hath the witness in himself," can make Revelation less precious to us. If any are disposed to say, "Surely *once* we see light in God's light, Revelation must become less needful to our peace;" there is a sense in which this is true:—but what would the state of mind be which would arise if doubts as to the divine authority of Scripture could be combined with certainty as to the truth received through Scripture? Such a combination is impossible, because that inherent certainty which belongs to divine light establishes beyond all other evidence, and independent of all other evidence, the Inspiration of the Scriptures through which that light has been received: but were it otherwise—were it possible to entertain the thought that what has revealed God and has led to God, was yet not from God—how utterly and painfully perplexing would such a thought be! But as there is no place for such a thought, any pain that actually can be felt by the believer having "the witness in himself," can only arise from the fear of the possible sealing up to others of what has been as a fountain of living water to his own spirit—and whatever tends to this he must resist to the utmost of his power. But the excitement to which I refer has quite another character, and indicates, not personal peace in God, and the desire to keep open for others the path to the same peace, but an uncertain hold of God, and a sensitiveness which implies that those in whom it appears have not the witness in themselves of which the Apostle speaks, but are, in inexperience of divine teaching, clinging to a mere traditional faith.

2. Another indication of the absence of faith in the Inspiration of the Divine Life is presented to us in the history of religious opinions and controversies. To bring what offends us in this history forward as an objection to the Inspiration of Revelation is unjust; seeing that, whatever lawless and unfettered thought men have given place to in studying the Bible, while its Inspiration has been fully recognised, anything that tends to lower our conception of its Inspiration can have no other tendency than to increase the evil. But the great cause, both of the endless diversity of religious opinion, and of the frequent uncharitableness and bitterness of religious controversy, is, the want of faith in the abiding presence of the Holy Spirit with the Church as our

individual teacher. Not that this faith would preclude altogether diversity in our measures of light. Were we all what scholars in the school of Christ should be, the degree of our progress would still vary. Without questioning the soundness of the way in which they were seeking divine light, the Apostle recognises different measures of attainment—some able to see eye to eye with him, some not yet able—but because they were proceeding in the right way, he says, "If in any thing ye be otherwise minded, God shall reveal even this unto you."[1] If we keep in view the difference between the Inspiration of Revelation and the Inspiration of the Divine Life, we shall see that there must be diversity in the measure in which the students of the Bible enter into its teaching. If it was through "being rooted and grounded in love" that the Ephesians were to be "able to comprehend with all saints what is the breadth and length and depth and height, and to know the love of Christ which passeth knowledge," the measure of their love would be the measure of their comprehension. But any diversity that would thus arise, would be very different from that which has arisen

[1] Phil. iii. 15.

from men's practical disregard of divine teaching, and forgetfulness of the moral and spiritual nature of religious truth,—the relation of light in this region to love. For thus the Bible has been read as any authoritative treatise or law-book might be read, men setting themselves by the mere exercise of intelligence in comparing passages and collating texts, to ascertain doctrines as the elements of a creed, and to gather rules of life for practical guidance: as if such knowledge of doctrines were enough to raise us to the knowledge of the living God, or as if mere rules of life could help us to fellowship in the life of the Son of God. We easily see that the study of spiritual truth in this forgetfulness of its spiritual nature, must be attended with a risk of wandering into speculative thought through not coming into contact with spiritual realities—a risk not unlike that to which scientific speculation was exposed, and from which it suffered before the obligation of coming into contact with facts in inductive investigation was understood.

But it is not in the diversity of opinion which has arisen, that the absence of faith in divine teaching is to be seen, so much as in the mere play of intellect and confidence in argument, and assumption of a right to demand assent on the strength of a mere logical conclusion, which marks religious controversy as much as it does controversy in any other field of human thought and mental conflict. No man who knows something higher in the history of his own religious convictions than a mere exercise of his intelligence,—who knows that seeking in prayer and self-negation to be strengthened by the Holy Spirit to see in the divine light of love, he has reached whatever consciousness he has of seeing light in God's light,—can expect to bring another to see eye to eye with him by dint of argument or collating of texts, or can feel any freedom to triumph in his use of controversial weapons, or to taunt men with blindness if they will not see what he puts plainly before them.

But there is more and worse than this. Religious controversies not only wear all the features of the intellectual encounter of minds, like other controversies; they, alas! too often shew that if all is not cold lifeless intellect, if there is a life present also with its own proper interest and feelings, that life is not the divine life, but the life of the flesh. We marvel and may well marvel, how it was possible that spiritual gifts could in the Corinthian Church have been valued as ministering to vanity and the sense of self-importance,—how even in that high spiritual region knowledge could puff up. But the Apostle explains this to us when he assumes that spiritual gifts may be without charity. And this is also the explanation of a corresponding marvel among ourselves—a great marvel, though, it may be, not so great, but still what its commonness alone prevents us from wondering at;—namely, that discussions about the truth of God, which ought to take their character and tone from their subject, and would do so were they entered into in the strength of the Holy Spirit, are defaced and deformed by the unseemly outbreaking of self-love.

It is not our faith in the Inspiration of the Bible that has made the history of religious thought and religious controversy that history of confusion and discord with which we are reproached. How could that faith possibly lead to such a result? On the contrary, must it not have been some restraint? and would it not have been a strong restraint, had it been more real, and had the conviction that it was the meaning of words of God which men were enquiring into been a more living conviction? But the real cause has been, that the Bible has been studied like an ordinary book, irrespective of the promise of the Spirit, and this because our need of the Spirit has not been felt—because it has not been felt that "the natural man receiveth not the things of the Spirit of God: for they are foolishness unto him: neither can he know them because they are spiritually discerned."[1]

3. But apart from what has been evil in the history of religious controversies, the unbelief which we are considering has injuriously affected religious thought. The fatal error of forgetting the spiritual nature of our employment and our consequent dependence on the Spirit of God for success, may be traced influencing our quietest and most earnest solitary study of the Bible; giving a wrong direction to our expectation of light, and causing us to draw on the intellect for that which the mere intellect has not to give;— though being received from the Spirit of God, it takes up the intellect and fills its highest capacity. And thus, just as men seeking righteousness by the law, and not by faith, attained not to righteousness, so men seeking the apprehension of divine light by the mere intellect, and not by

[1] 1 Cor. ii. 14.

the aid of the Spirit of God, attain not to that apprehension; and the highest truths of Revelation are either rejected, or held as mere doctrines, remaining unknown as spiritual realities. Thus the great foundation truth of the Atonement is so often either rejected as unbelievable, or accepted as a fact which is not to be understood; its nature being assumed to be as much veiled from men as if either it had not been accomplished by the Son of God *in humanity*, or that we for whose salvation it has been wrought had not been called to participation in the *divine nature* nor endowed with the Holy Spirit, and so made capable of apprehending the divine work of Him who "through the eternal Spirit offered Himself without spot to God." We remain in darkness through want of faith in the Spirit of truth, who guides to all truth; and we hide our unbelief from ourselves, by calling it humility and distrust of our own understanding. But intellectual pride rejecting what it cannot understand, and blind faith, in prostration of the intellect, accepting implicitly a traditional creed, are equally opposed to that faith which is the result of being taught of God, and in His light seeing light clearly: and so all measures of Infidelity and Superstition, as well as all dry dogmatic thought, no less than the great divergence of religious opinions, and the unspiritual character of religious controversies, testify how far the Christian Church, whose special calling it is to be a living witness for the fulfilment of the promise of the Spirit, is practically wanting in faith in that promise, however it remains an article in our creeds.

4. But these indications of unbelief as to the Inspiration of the Divine Life, may be admitted and condemned, while yet the extent of the evil is not understood. Misgivings and anxious fears as to men's hold of truth, manifested in the presence of attacks on the evidences of Christianity—all that is matter of reproach in the history of religious opinions and religious controversies—the limitation of the hope of light to what mere intelligence can attain, leading to the rejection of Divine Truth, or the reception of it as mere doctrine in contented spiritual darkness and false humility;—these evils are all on the surface. The root evil is a shortcoming in our ideal of Christianity.

We have seen that of the two Inspirations present in the Apostles—that of Revelation and that of the Divine Life—that which has ceased was less than that which remains;—gifts being less than charity, divine revelations less than the divine life to which they minister:—nay, that divine light in the highest sense of these words is not imparted by the Inspiration of Revelation, but is limited to divine life,—*the true and ultimate knowledge of God who is love being limited to those who dwell in love.* To this height do the words rise, "the secret of the Lord is with them that fear Him." God therefore has not withdrawn from any nearness to man, into which we conceive Him to have ever come. The greatest nearness to God into which Apostles were ever brought, was that to which they were raised when they had "fellowship with the Father and with His Son Jesus Christ;" and to this nearness to God —to fellowship in this fellowship—they have called us by the Gospel. "That which we have seen and heard declare we unto you, that ye also may have fellowship with us: and truly our fellowship is with the Father and with His Son Jesus Christ."[1]

The abundant development of the Divine Life which we see in the Apostles, is therefore the

[1] 1 John i. 3.

constant witness to us of what we are ourselves called to be. But we cannot be occupied with what we see these men as Apostles, without having our thoughts sent back to what we knew them as Disciples: and when we consider how their feeble dawn has brightened into day, we remember their Lord's words to them, when as He spoke to them of His going away, "sorrow filled their hearts:" "Nevertheless I tell you the truth: it is expedient for you that I go away: for if I go not away, the Comforter will not come unto you; but if I depart, I will send Him unto you."[1] The Comforter promised has come to them, and it is seen to have been indeed expedient for them that their Lord went away; for their whole position in relation to the kingdom of God is now advanced—they are raised to a higher level. Spiritually, they have received Him back again who had gone away from them, now to know Him better than before, now to have communion with Him in the abundant fellowship of His own divine love, the love of God being shed abroad in their hearts by the Holy Ghost. The extent of the change in the condition of these

[1] St. John xvi. 7.

men, through the fulfilment of their Lord's promise to send them the Comforter, I need not picture further. We are all familiar with it—so far as words can make us so. How deeply does it concern us to realise *how* this change has come to pass—that it is indeed the work of the Holy Spirit in them! For the Apostles are not alone on this higher level to which we see them raised. They are only the foremost figures and the leading men in the company of the faithful seen sharing with them in this Inspiration of the Divine Life, as what belongs to the common salvation: and we know that what is thus seen in humanity was meant to continue;—that we are not looking at an opening in the heavens revealing to us a bright vision of angels praising God, that we are looking at men of like passions with ourselves, in whom is seen the fruit of the death of Christ for our sins, and of His being raised again for our justification. That which we see we are called ourselves to be, through being, as those we look at, living temples of the Holy Ghost.

Is this then the true ideal of Christianity? Has the divine purpose for man, which had run through the preceding ages, been so far realised in the Early Church as to leave us no room for uncertainty as to that nearness of God to man which divine love has contemplated, and which accords with, and which alone accords with, the Incarnation and the Atonement and the presence of the risen Saviour in humanity at the right hand of the Father, having all power in Heaven and on Earth, and with our part in all He has done, and in all He is, according to the divine constitution of humanity in Him? Yes. This is in very truth the divine ideal for man—the love of God perfected in man; and we cannot receive all else that our creed embraces and refuse to acknowledge it as such.

There is no proportion between the divine *means* and the divine *end* otherwise. We may as well give up the faith and hope of the eternal inheritance itself as a fruit of redemption, as give up our part in the present earnest of the inheritance. If "when He who is our life shall appear, we shall appear with Him in glory," we know that this shall be by the power of the living God "according to the working of His mighty power which He wrought in Christ when He raised Him from the dead, and set Him at His own right hand in heavenly places;" and this power is the same that is spoken of as "the exceeding greatness of His power to usward who believe."[1]

If Christianity cannot be realised in us apart from our relation to the Father and the Son, no more can it apart from our relation to the Holy Spirit. If our relation to God were only what is expressed by saying that He gave us existence and upholds us in being, and if this were all that is meant by speaking of Him as our Father, and of ourselves as His offspring, there would be in this nothing to make participation in the divine nature essential to our occupying aright our place in God's universe. But sonship, as it is revealed in the Son of God and is given to us in Him, is not mere derived and dependent existence. Participation in the divine nature is manifestly of its very essence. We cannot conceive of it as a conscious life otherwise than as a life in the Holy Spirit. For *this* sonship we learn to see and know in that life of Christ which is the light of men. Our attention is fixed upon it in its relation to ourselves by the voice from Heaven which says of Jesus, "This is my beloved Son in whom I am well pleased; hear ye Him."[2] And though the visibility of this life of sonship,

---

[1] Eph. i. 19, 20.   [2] St. Matt. xvii. 5.

to those to whom these words—ever addressed to us in the Spirit—were originally addressed by an audible voice from Heaven, is but imperfectly pictured in the record of our Lord's life on earth, we learn enough from this record to understand the high character of that sonship as communion with the Father, hearing His voice, abiding in His love, and therefore only to be known in the Holy Spirit. What spiritual recognition of it the disciples reached in their near personal intercourse with the Son of God, was, we know, due to divine teaching; while the fulness of knowledge which we see them subsequently manifesting, was through the power of the promised Comforter taking of the things of Christ and shewing them to them. We have our place in the kingdom of God in this its most advanced stage. We therefore are called to know and live the life of sonship, not as Old Testament saints, nor even as the disciples—while but the disciples —knew and lived it, but as the Apostles and Early Church knew and lived it after the risen Saviour had sent upon His Church the promise of the Father, that in the power of the Holy Ghost proceeding from the Father and the Son, they might be the sons of God in spirit and in truth.

Therefore do I say that the root evil, of which the indications of unbelief in the Inspiration of the Divine Life now noticed are but surface fruits, is shortcoming and inadequacy in our conception of Christianity. I have said that unconsciousness as to the gulf between the sure truth of Revelation and our having individually the assured knowledge of truth, has alone made it possible to study the Bible in hope of light, without reference to the personal teaching of the Holy Spirit. But our need is deeper, and the promise larger. The office of the Comforter is to take of the things that are Christ's and shew them to us. In doing this in connection with Revelation, He fills the written word with divine light to us; enabling us to know and see Christ in the Scriptures which testify of Him. But Christ is our life; and what we need is what the prayer of the Apostle for the Ephesians contemplates, namely, to "be strengthened with might by the Spirit in the inner man, that Christ may dwell in our hearts by faith;" and we know that even the spiritual understanding of revealed truth leaves us still dependent upon the living presence and power of the Holy Spirit for all actual fellowship in the life of the Son of God.

It is realising this that we understand how their relation to the Holy Spirit was to the Apostolic Church what we see it to have been.

But all that we thus know of the grace of God to man in this dispensation of the Spirit as realised by the Apostles, and by those who were followers of them as they of the Lord Jesus, we can see to be contained in those words of communion with the Father which precede our Lord's gracious invitation to us as the weary and heavy-laden to come to Him for rest. "All things are delivered unto me of my Father: and no man knoweth the Son but the Father; neither knoweth any man the Father save the Son, and he to whomsoever the Son will reveal Him."[1] These words reveal the Divine circle into which we have to be taken up, that the love of God may accomplish its desire in us. We are to know the Son by the teaching of the Father: we are to know the Father by the teaching of the Son. The Father drawing us to the Son, the Son revealing the Father;—these are Divine actings in the Holy Spirit. Reader, are we called to be the subjects of them—to experience them in ourselves? To know that this is so—that God's

[1] St. Matt. xi. 27.

love to us contemplates nothing less—is to know our relation to the Holy Spirit.

V.

There is in this day offered to us as the ultimate result of thought, a conception of man in his relation to this universe, which presents the most extreme contrast to that ideal of a divine life in God which the Gospel sets before us. Of that ideal I have now spoken, as what it is of vital importance to apprehend clearly, and keep steadfastly in view: for, as I have said above, the only protection from false Christs is the knowledge of the true. The merchantman still seeking goodly pearls may be attracted by the seeming beauty of what is not a true pearl: but *he* will not be thus deceived who has found the one Pearl of great price, and has so known its value, that he has sold all that he had and bought it. What is this that to many seems a goodly pearl—the sober philosophic truth of things— for which we are invited to give up Christianity as a poetic dream? What is it proposed to leave to us as real—what to take from us as having been but a fond imagination? I desire to consider these questions fairly, however great the pain they give: and it is no small help to fairness here, to remember that if any are tempted to slight the Christian solution of the great problem of our existence—whence and wherefore we are—what is the meaning of the life of man—what is man's true wisdom,—one cause of this is, that those who profess to accept that solution, appear little able practically to proceed on its truth, as on firm ground. Not that our weak faith will justify any in their rejection of light. Let God be true and every man a liar. Still the consciousness that we are not to others that help to faith which we ought to be, may well teach us patience in dealing with them.

What we, who believe that God has given us eternal life in His Son—that we are called to fellowship with the Father and the Son in the Spirit—are asked to accept in place of this faith is the so-called scientific result;—that either there is no God, or we are incapable of knowledge of Him, or if we may know anything of Him, it can be no more than that He is a first cause of things;—that, practically, we as intelligent thinking beings find ourselves in an universe which meets us at all points with fixed laws, which encompass us about externally, and rule us also within—fixed laws in the region of matter, fixed laws in the region of mind—that, therefore, knowledge to us is knowledge of laws, and can be nothing more; and that wisdom in us is simply the skill to turn our knowledge of these laws to the best account, conforming ourselves to them, and availing ourselves of them to appropriate to ourselves all the good they bring within our reach.

We refuse to accept the offer of a scientific solution of the great problem of man's life, because that problem does not lie within the domain of Science, but belongs to a higher region, and is to be dealt with in the exercise of a capacity of our being, higher than that which Science engages; and it appears due in fairness to place our refusal on this its proper footing: for laws are the domain of Science, a report of laws is all that mere Science can bring to us; it carries us in all directions up to a barrier of laws impassable to it. Doubtless it is a great and fundamental error to hold the physical world and the moral world as in *relation to God* different planes; so that they cannot be conceived of as combined in one scheme of government. Such an assumption not only precludes—as it has been employed to do—the conception of miracles as having a place in the history of religion, but precludes also all comfort in identifying the God of Nature and Providence with the moral sovereign Lord of the Universe—all comfort in knowing the Framer of our bodies as the Father of our spirits,—all warrant to connect sickness and pain with the wise discipline of divine love. But however great this error, which would empty the beauty of the lily of its lesson of faith and separate by so wide a space between the fall of a sparrow and our Father, in reference to *us* and our capacities of knowledge Science and Religion are not convergent, but parallel lines. Science prosecuted as Science, and in the exclusive exercise of the faculties which Science engages, cannot, however far-reaching and final its conclusions, lead us up to God. We are shocked with the state of mind expressed by him who said, that what he found in the scientific study of the starry heavens was the glory of Newton and his fellow-thinkers, and not the glory of God. We are rightly shocked: but it is because the utterer of these words was a man, and the starry heavens as declaring God's glory spoke to that in him which was higher than his scientific faculty—spoke to his spirit. We see him therefore living, though not in his lowest, yet, in his lower nature where man may glory in man. We know that the Hebrew shepherd, to whom the heavens declared the glory of God, saw with another and a higher mental vision than that which sees relations of space, and discovers laws of motion. As no telescope can enable us to see God, nor microscope to ascertain His presence and working,—as the motion of the living sap in a plant is made visible; so no chemistry by its analysis, were it even to reduce all substances to one simple elemental base,—no study of forces, were it to bring to an ideal perfection its theory of a protean force which is now motion and now heat, and now expansion and now muscular action—would bring us one hairbreadth nearer to God. Doubtless we justly trace to a spiritual origin in the sense of the unity of God, the interest and charm which all simplifying in Science has for us—all reducing of many causes to one. But while this is true, and however parallel the line of Science to that of Faith, *pursued in the abeyance of our spiritual nature Science attains not to God.* Nay, so pursued, it may and probably often does produce such states of mind as that to which, in the case above referred to, expression has been given in such man-glorifying words. To him who knows God all things are of God—Science as well as all else: but though his Faith takes up his Science and offers it in worship, glorifying God in it, it is not by Science that he knows God. So also when we would marvel that the higher Art does not lead men up to God, this is not because of limits to Art of man's own placing. Art, simply as Art, carried to its highest power would not reach God; though the artist being spiritual, his Art will be to him among the all things which are his with a true possession, because he is Christ's and Christ is God's. There is but one path to God. Jesus says, "I am the way, the truth, and the life: no man cometh unto the Father, but by me."[1]

I have said this much on this point, because it seems to me that we sometimes unconsciously leave our proper ground, and so are found contending for truth both at a disadvantage and unfairly. We attempt to show to men of Science, as being in Science itself, that which is, indeed,

[1] St. John xiv. 6.

and rightly, its highest interest to us, but which our faith has taken into it—not found in it. We are quite entitled to call upon them also as spiritual beings to take this higher interest into Science; but we are not justified in requiring them as mere men of Science to see it there. Let us then consider how this so-called scientific view affects the elements of our life and well-being. It brings us nothing: but what does it leave?—what is our loss in what it takes away?

It leaves to life physical, and intellectual, and social enjoyment. It leaves us Science and that Art which is the practical application of Science, and by which Science enlarges the sphere of our power over nature; it leaves us Art in the higher sense of the word—painting, sculpture, music, poetry; it leaves us social life—the relationships of husband and wife—parent and child—brother and sister—friendly fellowship in labour and in pleasure; it leaves us also self-executing moral laws, having power in themselves to reward obedience and to punish disobedience;—all these gifts it leaves though it takes away the great Giver. Great riches surely;—the portion of goods which fall to him, given to the prodigal, permitted to take them with him to the far country:—I enumerate them that I may be fair to error while rejecting it, and that no one who mistakes this error for light, and so walks in it, may be able to say, that this and that good thing he finds remaining to him, of which religious men had assumed that his being without God in the world would have deprived him. The intelligent and earnest study and observance of laws may be the path to a civilisation and culture of humanity which may look very goodly, so long as it is not taken to a higher light. There may be a subordinating of man's lowest nature to what is higher, a culture of the intellect and taste and affections, kindness responding to kindness; nay, there may be a culture of justice and benevolence, and a tasting of the pleasure proper to these—the law that whatsoever a man soweth he shall also reap, holding in the moral as well as in the physical world. This is difficult ground. In the desire to be fair and just, concessions not really due may be made. No society has existed in which morality has sustained itself without religion: and as to individual cases we would not, I believe, be warranted in accepting even men's own profession of infidelity, as evidence that *even in them* morality was cut off from God. I do not mean merely that we know that what suggests the right is of God, though men may not themselves recognise this. I mean that even where goodness is in a man's *theory* most cut off from God, strength for goodness, rest in goodness is to be referred to the deep *instinct* that goodness is supreme.

But, assuming all that can be held to be theoretically possible, however little actually realised—assuming that the gifts of God may furnish life with much varied and even refined and in itself not unworthy interest apart from faith, what is the highest ideal thus conceivable when taken to the light of the divine ideal revealed in Christ? I desire to keep to the soberness of speech which accords with the greatness and solemnity of the subject—not yielding to the deep feelings which it awakens. Let the light of the divine love which has been shut out be supposed to flow in upon God's varied gifts, and let us endeavour to conceive the change. No gift, however low in the scale, is to us so much simply in itself, as it comes to be when received from our Father's hand—a gift of love; the love which had imparted the capacity to which the gift is suited now bestowing the gift. But as to lower gifts, faith does not change what they are in themselves. The lily was not less fragrant, nor the rose less beautiful, while not yet enjoyed in faith; though now they are no longer a mere lily and a mere rose, but divine words to our spirits. But as we ascend upwards, the greatness of the difference becomes more and more marked, the very nature and inherent value of the gift being affected. Parental instinct, for example, needs not the living sense of God's Fatherliness for its existence or its development, as an intense interest and sweet element of life. Yet in the light of God's Fatherliness how is the whole relation raised to be a higher gift! The power of the parental instinct to interpret Divine Fatherliness, when the welling up of the one in the heart is combined with believing contemplation of the other, imparts to this instinct an inestimable additional value. Besides, there is the higher light in which the child is seen as one of God's offspring—the dignity imparted to the parental relation as a type of the higher Fatherhood of the Father of spirits—the future for the child to which faith and hope look forward—the inheritance in Christ to which it is born, and for which it is the parent's appointed task and labour of love to educate it;—these all are to be taken into account here,—for to unbelief these exist not. No relationship needs more an open path up to God than that of parent and child, if, realising what human life is, the parent is to cherish with a free mind and peaceful hope his instinctive interest in his offspring. Laws, including the highest and the best—what can they promise to the parent's heart, cut off from Him Whose goodness they embody, Whose Will they reveal, and Whose interest in, and purpose for, the child they so far express?

Passing from this inmost point of care for a life derived from oneself, let us go to the outer circle of social existence. The well-being of the many around him, is a question of little interest to the individual man, while absorbed in gross selfishness. But we have instincts which bind man to man, as well as parent to child; and even while not living the higher life we may be under the power of these instincts,—as men being evil may give good gifts to their children. The interest which man is to man is so proper to humanity, that its absence is justly termed "inhumanity:" and those who acknowledge no higher social cement than natural laws, would feel that injustice was done to their theory if such a law as this was not recognised. I believe they deceive themselves in regard to the extent of the power for good of this or any other element of goodness, while God is not acknowledged. But could there be a true development of the instinct of human brotherhood in which the Fatherhood of God had no part, what would be the result? How would the human spirit bear the weight of the multitude of brothers? Is it not the case of the parent and child multiplied? The man who could thus receive others into his heart, and bear them on his spirit without liberty to cast the burden of his interest in them on God in faith, would be of all men most miserable. For looking at men as they are, what hope is there from the existence and fixedness of moral and spiritual laws, if there be not One who is dealing with men to bring them into conformity with these laws?

But could true brotherhood be known while the Father remained unknown? The kindly instincts of humanity we know greatly modify our social existence, even while self still continues the root of life; but can the root of love be substituted for the root of self, otherwise than according to the divine order and the relation of the second commandment to the first? Can man be his own centre, and love his neighbour as himself? Can a man cease to be his own centre otherwise than in God's becoming his centre? Is it assumed that love being understood,—its beauty and its preeminent dignity as the highest law being known,—it will be welcomed for what it is, and that thus the individual man may yield himself to it, and become blest while yet no personal God is known, who *is love* and who is the fountain of love? Is it assumed that divine light may thus visit us and save us without revealing the Father of lights from whom it comes? This may not be. The light shining in darkness while the darkness comprehends it not—pulsations of the divine life in us while we know not yet Him who is our life—the sap of the vine pressing into the branch while it is not yet revealed to it that it is but a branch, that Christ is the Vine,—may cause experiences which, not rightly interpreted, may produce godless dreams of good; and instead of leading men to God, the fountain of life, in whose light they may see light, may cause the proud illusion that they are fountains of light and life themselves; but this is all. Such broken glimpses of light thus misunderstood bring no deliverance. "He that dwelleth in love dwelleth in God, and God in him." This is the history of man's dwelling in love: it can have no other.

Therefore we conclude that to empty life of God, is to empty it of man also, in respect to that highest value which man has to man, viz. the value which he has in the eyes of love; and that we use no mere specious form of speech, but utter a sure truth of the highest moment, when we say, that to look up and see no Father, is to look around and see no brother. Such is the solitude of pure self—that self to which we must die that we may live to God and to man. "Except a grain of wheat die it abideth alone."

We might well draw back from the teaching that would rob us of God our Father, even if the only objection were, that in so doing it will rob us of men our brethren. But the words "rob us of God our Father" demand themselves our first attention, and have an import which no thought of ours can adequately embrace, nor words of ours express. Men value religion because it exalts and purifies the social life of man with man, rather than as *itself a life in communion with God.* This is to forget that " the first and great commandment is, " Thou shalt love the Lord thy God with all thy heart, and with all thy soul, and with all thy mind."[1] The divine purpose is that God should be Himself the great interest which is to fill the utmost capacity of our being. As the Psalmist says (Psa. cxxxix.) of God's knowledge of us, " It is high, I cannot attain unto it," so we feel as to the claim on our love which God makes, that we cannot fully grasp the thought of it; it is so all-embracing, proposing to take us up so entirely, leaving no part of us free, or that we may bestow otherwise than on God. Such a claim is either very terrible or very joyful—according as we hear it as the Law or as the Gospel—in the flesh or in the spirit. Heard apart from Christ, in the clear cold light of a demand made on us by Him from whom we derive existence, and our dependence upon whom is necessary, absolute and eternal, this claim is very terrible. Heard in the light of Christ who reveals the Father, and in whom we have power to be the sons of God in spirit and in truth, it is very joyful—the

[1] St. Matt. xxii. 37.

Gospel of our salvation. In meditating on the divine knowledge of us as the Psalmist helps us to do, we feel that the faith of God's "precious thoughts" for us enables us to "welcome God's searching eye,"—yea, to pray that God may "search us and know our heart, try us and know our thoughts, and see if there be any wicked way in us, and lead us in the way everlasting." So also here, when we see the claim for love which God makes in the light of the knowledge of the power to respond to it which we have in Christ, this claim is to us the gracious invitation to enjoy our divine inheritance; for our inheritance is God Himself. It may be said that everything which God gives us, He gives by giving the capacity of enjoying whatever excellence is in it; as He gives the landscape by giving us the eye that sees it, and the mental eye that takes in its beauty. So God gives Himself to us in giving us the capacity of knowing and enjoying what He is. Among God's gifts the highest are what we possess by love, that is to say, persons. Of this all human life is the perpetual illustration: so that "if a man would give all the substance of his house for love, it would utterly be contemned." God gives Himself in giving us the power to possess Him as the *treasure of the heart*—the capacity of loving Him with a *personal love*. Assuming that we can love God, what He will be to us will be according to the fitness to be loved which is in God, and the measure in which the capacity of loving Him is developed in us.

We need have no difficulty in distinguishing between what through love God comes to be to us, and all the other elements of our well-being. He is the Giver of good gifts, and He is much to us because of their value to us; but we are accustomed in other relations to distinguish between the value which any gift has in itself, and the value which the love which gives the gift, has to us for its own sake and as love. What must the love of God discerned in all things and responded to in love become to us! Here the addition which a loving father is to the family life of a household, as distinct from all they get from him, is an obvious as it is also a fair illustration; and may help the man, who would make our life in our personal relation to God a blank, to understand what the void in life would be which he would thus cause. But we must take him up to a higher region than that in which God is known as giving gifts which we distinguish from the Giver, if we would shew to him what God is to us—even to that region in which God is at once the Giver and the Gift. In Christ it is Himself that God gives to man: and to understand this, is to understand what would be taken out of the life of a Christian man by making his personal relation to God a blank, and leaving him with an environment of mere laws.

Finally, it is not the measure in which any one of us is proving in his own experience God's unspeakable gift, that is here to be considered. This gift is indeed more to the feeblest faith, which accepts it truly, than we ourselves know: yet to the strongest faith, it is infinitely less than it is in itself. And the real question is, what is it in itself? Even in giving us to each other, God is giving more than we ever receive. How much more is this true in regard to God's giving Himself to us! In the fairest specimens of family or social life, no relationship is ever so lived, as to realise the ideal of that relationship. So also we never approach, but at an immeasurable distance, to the divine ideal of sonship presented to our faith: "This is my beloved Son in whom I am well pleased. Hear ye Him."

I have now, as I proposed, offered to the reader's attention a few elemental thoughts on Inspiration—both the Inspiration of Revelation and that of the Divine Life; and this with special reference to the two opposite tendencies manifested at present—on the one hand, to see in the former only a higher degree of the latter; on the other hand, to disregard the latter in a way of trust in that fruit of the former which we possess in the Bible: I have added as what seems to me a conclusion suited to the need of our time, a brief consideration of that so-called scientific theory of life which assigns to fixed laws of existence the place which we give to God, and which substitutes as the highest hope for man the power which knowledge of these fixed laws will bring, for the power to be the sons of God which the Gospel reveals as given to us in the Son of God.

I have placed what is offered as the scientific theory of the universe in immediate contrast with faith in the living God in its highest form. It is in contemplating two opposite principles in their extreme development, that what they severally are becomes most clear to us. I believe the contrast now drawn is fitted to be profitable in confirming faith. But I believe that it is also what it is wise to present to the attention of thoughtful minds still suffering from unbelief. As the elemental faith that God is "a rewarder of them that diligently seek Him," is seen in Christianity in its full development both as to the "seeking" and the "reward;" so is it as thus fully developed that we must present this faith to men in order that the divine demand for it may have its highest justification. It may seem a paradox to hold that the highest demand for faith is the most easily met. Yet it is not difficult to understand that to fix attention on the ultimate result is, in the case of a thoughtful mind determined to count the costs, the likely way of soonest bringing it to the conviction that the kingdom of God is worth that price of "all that we have" which God has put upon it. The highest faith is, that God has given to us eternal life in His Son—that because we are sons, God sends forth the Spirit of His Son into our hearts, crying Abba Father.[1] This is a faith as to ourselves which seems much more difficult than that

[1] Gal. iv. 6.

which is called for by that lower conception of our relation to God, according to which, to speak of ourselves as God's offspring, means only that we derive existence from God—and are distinguished from lower creatures of God by the capacity of knowing that this is so, and of understanding that it is due from us to use life according to the will and purpose of the Great Giver, and with thanksgiving. But if we consider what this simpler, and as may be thought less mystical language really means, asking ourselves "what will be a sure knowledge of God and of His will?" and "what response from our hearts will correspond with our obligations to God?" it will be felt that it is more easy to believe our high relation to God in Christ, and accept the solution of these questions which that relation offers, than to deal with the same questions on a lower level. For, however in ignorance of the state of their hearts towards God, the heedless and unreflecting may easily concede the obligation to love and serve God, earnest and truthful men must take up the question, "What provision has God made for our knowing Him with a true knowledge, and loving Him with a true love?" To such questions the Gospel as proclaimed to us in this dispensation of the Spirit offers the fullest answer: for in the light of the Grace of God in which we stand, we see that there is no limit to the knowledge of God and love to God to which our hopes may rise. But apart from the filling up of the measure of that Grace in the Inspiration of the Divine Life, I know not how "knowing God," "loving God," "delighting in God," are conditions of spirit to which we can expect to attain.

VI.

Men speak of the "mental initiative" needed for the true understanding of any counsel of wisdom, and our Lord recognises this need when He says, "Wisdom is justified of her children." In considering the ways of God in relation to man, the divine love which contemplates our knowing God as our Father and our being to Him dear children, is what we have to keep steadily before us as what is to interpret all things. Thus we read, "it became Him, for Whom are all things, and by Whom are all things, in bringing many sons unto glory, to make the Captain of their salvation perfect through sufferings."[1] We are not to shrink from the words "it became Him," as if *we* could not be justified in using them in relation to the ways of God. The truth is, we cannot help attempting to use them. What we have to watch against is using them rashly. I have, in the former part of what is here written, endeavoured to take the three distinctly marked conditions of mind which exist in relation to divine truth—Superstition, Infidelity, and Faith—to the light of the love of God to man; concluding that Faith alone accords with this love. In the same light of the divine purpose, we arrive at satisfying conclusions on the subject of Inspiration, both the Inspiration of Revelation and that of the Divine Life; as well as of all else in which the kingdom of nature is made subordinate to the kingdom of grace. When it is asked, "Can the interruption of the sublime order of nature be a higher witness for God than that order itself?" we are thankful for the light in which we can answer, "Not higher, but more fitted for the end contemplated." If "the invisible things of God be not understood by the things that are made, even His eternal power and Godhead," the Supernatural

---

[1] Heb. ii. 10.

will not reveal God. But in the light of the will of God to make Himself personally known to us, and to cherish in us the sense of our personal relation to Him, the whole history of God's coming near to the chosen people, and of the self-manifestation by which He made Himself known to them, becomes easy of belief. So, as to the kindred question, "Why should so much important knowledge in other departments be reached by man in the exercise of his natural faculties alone, and knowledge in the region of religion have a supernatural history?" we are able to see, not only that the nature of the knowledge to be imparted has necessitated this, but that it accords with the whole end of imparting it that it should be bestowed in this way, and not as other knowledge is given. If a science of theology were contemplated, there would be nothing in the idea of such a science—I mean apart from the character of the divine facts to be made known—to call for this difference. But the end contemplated being Religion—a living bond between God and man—it was most fitting that in the very conveying of the knowledge needed, God should be revealed as seeking man. How different the position of Moses coming to the people from God—God also bearing him witness and confirming his testimony—from the position which he would have occupied had he come to them offering results of his own researches into divine things!—how different, I mean, as to bringing the living God near to the people. The very form in which the call to faith and worship came, was itself a help to faith and worship. The words "Thus saith the Lord" in the mouth of a prophet, declared the loving jealous care of God as no mere human words of counsel or rebuke or warning could. When God sent Nathan to David, there was, as to the substance of his message, nothing which David might not have heard spoken within him by conscience—nothing which he did not come afterwards to hear so spoken; neither was the moral rebuke other than what a wise and faithful friend might have addressed to him. But how impossible is it not to feel the peculiar power to quicken in David the faith of the holy love that was marking his path and condemning his sin, which there was in *God's sending* Nathan to him! Take this element from the narrative, and how much is taken away of the help to David's spirit to come to that better mind in which he said,

"Against thee, thee only have I sinned, and done this evil in thy sight."

It does not appear that there was usually anything to command faith for the divine message by a Prophet beyond trust in his truthfulness and the response in the hearts of those addressed; although this response could not of course reach to definite prophetic intimations, whether promises or denunciations, or referring to a near or a distant future: these rather demanded faith than helped it. But men were prepared to be spoken to through Prophets; and it agreed with the character in which the Prophet spoke, speaking in the Name of the Lord, that the light shed on the present should reveal the future also—being His light who saves men from the evil power of the present by the hope of the glory to be revealed—the hope of righteousness. But, though not in attestation of what God spoke by them, we know that some at least of the Prophets wrought miracles; and that, besides the mighty works which God did by the hand of Moses, when at the first separating the nation of Israel to be to Himself a peculiar people, there were from time to time divine acknowledgments of faith in individual men, corresponding with what is written, "According to the word that I covenanted with you when ye came out of Egypt, so my spirit remaineth among you."[1] Such acts of faith, with the divine acknowledgment of them, have a high value as part of the history of man in his relation to God. So regarded, they are in themselves a revelation teaching *directly* faith in God. And with this agrees the use made of the history of the cloud of witnesses in the Epistle to the Hebrews (xi., xii. 1), and the reference to the divine acknowledgment of the faith of Elias by St. James (v. 17.) In this view we must regret the exclusive use of miracles as evidences of religion; leading to such questions as, "Does the miracle prove the doctrine, or the doctrine commend the miracle?" We may in answer say, that they mutually commend each other, and are in their harmony a twofold cord. We must also feel that they are so entwined in the Bible, that to deny the miracles must bring the divine origin of the doctrines into question, however strong the divine impress on them may be, because of the untruthfulness which would thus be stamped on the channel through which they have come to

---

[1] Haggai ii. 5.

us: while to detect in the doctrines what made them unworthy of God would be to disprove the miracles, that is, would be to separate between them and God; though they might still remain as recorded facts, indicating superhuman power. But such questions, although natural in connection with the chief use which we have made of miracles, would not occur to us using them simply as helps to faith in God. At the same time it would be untrue to our own experience to deny the increased authority which both the miracle and the doctrine have in their combination, each adding a certain prestige to the other; while each must be felt to be what it is in itself, that we may have the full experience of their combined power. Before faith was raised to a higher apprehension of His personal dignity, our Lord was recognised as "a Prophet mighty in deed and word"—by deed and by word witnessing for the Father. This He was "before all the people," and even to those to whom it was not given as to the Twelve to see more nearly the Father in Him. When He by the finger of God did mighty works, and gracious as well as mighty, the kingdom of God was brought nigh unto men; but we do not believe that the authority with which He spoke, constraining the testimony, "Never man spake like this man," owed anything of its power over men to the fact that He that spoke also wrought miracles. We indeed feel little of the response which His words should awaken, if their authority to us in reading them is not *immediate* and *direct*.

As our Lord's works were done in the name of the Father, so those of the Apostles were done in His name, and proclaimed the risen Saviour at the right hand of the Father, having all power in heaven and on earth. This is their distinctive character. The great miracle of Pentecost, indeed, declared the resurrection and exaltation of Christ *immediately*. "Therefore being by the right hand of God exalted, and having received of the Father the promise of the Holy Ghost, He hath shed forth this which ye now see and hear."[1] Here the Apostle was but an interpreter, not an actor, being but one of the subjects of the divine acting. But the words "Jesus Christ maketh thee whole"[2] equally raise faith direct to Christ—the power put forth in His name, itself teaching faith in Him, and not merely putting a seal to the teaching which it accom-

---

[1] Acts ii. 33. [2] Ibid. ix. 34.

panied. For faith in God—or in Christ at the right hand of God—*receiving the divine acknowledgment*, is thenceforth *a ground of faith to men for all time.*

But the record of their experience who trusted in God and were not put to shame, cannot help our faith unless the distinctive character of that experience is kept in view. And here a temptation may meet us—not indeed in our actual walk with God, but in our contendings for the faith— a temptation to endeavour to disarm the opposition of men of mere science by expressing *our* faith in *their* language. If all that is meant by speaking of miracles as "the manifestation of a higher law" is, *that it is a law of the kingdom of God—a principle on which God acts—to acknowledge trust in God by a direct response from God, or trust in Christ by a direct response from Christ*, then the thing said is true: but the use of the word "law" is here equivocal and misleading. What the man of science means by a law is what may be known and acted upon without any reference to God at all—something on which an atheist may calculate —*not* a law of the divine mind, proceeding on which we can contemplate doing something *through God*, as we contemplate doing a thing through a man whom we can trust to serve us.

The essential idea here is *the interposition of trust in God, and a response to that trust on God's part, between the will to do and the thing done.* This is altogether to be distinguished from availing ourselves of the fixedness of a law,—however true it is that faith will recognise the power of God in all laws. When our Lord at the grave of Lazarus "lifted up his eyes, and said, Father, I thank thee that thou hast heard me,"[1] we are made to know the direct trust in the Father through which it came to pass that the words "Lazarus come forth" were obeyed. Some one has said, "that we shall come to see that everything is a miracle, and that nothing is a miracle." If this means that we shall come to see the hand of God in all things—His present working—to this faith we desire to attain. But in the light of the fullest all-embracing faith the distinctive character of works wrought *by faith* will remain. Our missionaries avail themselves of medical science to win the attention and confidence of the heathen. They may freely use such a power for expressing kindly interest, and even as giving the prestige of higher knowledge; but they must not cease to realise the difference between their

[1] St. John xi. 41.

own position and that of those who preached Christ at the beginning. So to do would be to take a false position with the heathen; whilst it would also be a confounding of things which differ to their own serious loss. As to the heathen, a missionary cannot offer the healing which he accomplishes as a *proof* that Christ is exalted at the right hand of the Father, any more than the power of the bread they eat to feed them or of the air they breathe to sustain life. As to himself, however truly, in healing by the use of medicine, he may in his own spirit acknowledge God,— doing this as he is called to do all things "in the name of the Lord Jesus,"—he will greatly deceive himself if he confounds the faith which he is thus exercising, with that in which St. Peter said to the lame man who was laid at the Beautiful Gate of the Temple, "In the name of Jesus Christ of Nazareth rise up and walk."[1]

The distinction which I seek to mark is that between doing anything *in* faith, and doing it *by* faith: but I am not to be understood as depreciating the former attitude of spirit towards God, nor as denying that, being true and living, it is an honouring of God no less than the latter. There

[1] Acts iii. 6.

is, indeed, a practical difference which deserves attention in the fact that there is an opening for self-deception when no result tests faith—because no result depends upon it, which does not exist when the faith, if real, is sealed by the divine acknowledgment. But it is clear that to the person exercising faith, the consciousness of faith is its own witness, whether he is simply recognising God in what God is doing, or is trusting God to do that which he has asked Him to do. The important thing is that contemplative faith, however high its vision and the praise it gives to God, may be regarded as *only the faith that God is;* while faith trusting God and looking for a result from trusting God *adds* to the faith that God is, the faith that He is *a rewarder of them that diligently seek Him.* This latter element in the faith without which it is impossible to please God, I have recognised above as lying at the root of personal religion, and the real essence of our subject of controversy with all theists who deny that we are called to cultivate a personal relation with God: and it is in this view that the record of acts of trust in God which have received the divine acknowledgment, is so valuable an element in the sacred Scriptures. We meet some who feel that they would find it more easy to accept Revelation if it made no demand for faith in the Supernatural, at least in the region of physical laws. Could those who so feel accept the facts, being duly authenticated, instead of concluding beforehand against their possibility —a conclusion which of course precludes inquiry —they might be attracted by them and not repelled. At least we might hope for this in the case of any who are struggling against the temptation to lose the living God in laws; more especially if the divine purpose to cultivate in us personal trust in God, has commended itself to them as what is worthy of God.

The distinction between contemplative faith and that faith which is active trust expecting results from trusting—the former expressing itself in praise, the latter in prayer—we realise in our experience of the Inspiration of the Divine Life, in which *both* are called for in their highest measure. Praise has its highest meaning as man's acknowledgment of God when it is the utterance of a spirit "beholding the glory of God in the face of Jesus Christ." Prayer has its highest meaning when it deals with the living God in the faith of "the exceeding greatness of

His power to usward who believe, according to the working of His mighty power, which He wrought in Christ when He raised Him from the dead and set Him at His own right hand in the heavenly places."[1] And the vision which moves to praise and the promise which moves to prayer are so related that we pass naturally from the one to the other, the faith which apprehends the divine glory sustaining the faith which lays hold of the divine strength.

We know that trust in the living God in that which is purely spiritual is the highest trust, and has the highest results, being, indeed, that in which the *ultimate* end of God in calling us to faith is accomplished, namely, our living the divine life. Yet as the Jewish Church inherited from their fathers that help for faith in the living God which they possessed in the memory of the outstretched arm with which God took their nation out of Egypt, so we inherit, along with what they thus inherited, the record of our Lord's own mighty works, and of those mighty works which accompanied the founding of the Christian Church at the beginning. And the supernatural thus present in the Bible, is to all of us an ele-

[1] Eph. i. 19, 20.

ment in our faith. We have received it as *a part of that whole which the Bible is to us;* and this element in that whole has, according to its nature, told on our spirits in the measure in which we have been open to its fair influence: while our actual responsibility for faith has been—*the nature and character of that divine whole which in God's providential ordering of things has been presented for our faith.* I say its character in itself—the character of the miracles as well as of the doctrines; for the miracles as well as the doctrines have God's impress on them. On this character of that which claims their faith, and not on conclusions of historical criticism, the faith of the mass of men must ever rest: as on this also must depend the glory given to God in faith and the dishonour done to Him in unbelief. As to historical criticism it has had two voices; one in favour of faith, and one against faith. With the former we are more acquainted; while the latter has waxed louder and more confident of late: and now the former is again making itself heard, and new objections are receiving new answers. But the faith of simple men in accepting the former voice and refusing the latter, while unskilled to weigh perfectly the claims of either, is justified by the nature and character of that which is believed. But if we are to stand strong on this ground, we must not pervert the record of the Supernatural from its legitimate use; nor turn the eyes of our faith from the glory of God in the face of Jesus Christ to look at miracles as if the claim which that highest glory of God has on our faith rested on them. This has been the error of our carnal minds. I have already referred to the immediate authority which was in our Lord's teaching, which commended itself by what it was,—as His miracles also did by what they were.[1] So also as to the Apostle's divine teaching on the preeminent excellence of charity as compared with "the faith which could remove mountains," we feel that this teaching is not entering into the man who can say, "I believe what the Apostle teaches as to charity because he wrought miracles." It is doubtless sometimes nothing higher than difficulty in believing in the Supernatural which men express, when they say, that they can more easily bow as to what is divine to our Lord's Sermon on the Mount, or the Apostles' commendation of charity, than to any miracle however marvellous. But surely the

---

[1] St. Luke xi. 18, 19.

truly spiritual among those who believe the record as a whole, feel in the depths of their being, that these utterances of the divine mind—shinings forth of the divine light—lie more at the foundation of their faith than all miracles.

Recently, and also in times long past, some good men have not been able to rest satisfied with that record of the Supernatural, which, in the membership that is in Christ, makes us as to miracles debtors to those who have come before us; and so they have desired the manifestation of miraculous power now. This desire has doubtless been connected with the persuasion that in the absence of such manifestation the Church bears an imperfect testimony for her risen Lord. But it may also have arisen in part from the undue place which men have given to miracles in demanding faith for Christianity. It may be in mercy that what has been desired has been withheld, if much of this error has entered into the desire for it. Certainly no man would be in a state to witness the Supernatural with safety to his spiritual interests, who had made up his mind to believe whatever came to him with the seal of miracle;—a state of mind fitted to throw men open, *and which may eventually be found to have thrown them open*, to the assaults of error sealed by signs and lying wonders: while we know that the great power to teach men the faith that God has given to them eternal life in His Son, is, the manifest presence of that life in men of like passions with themselves. "That they all may be one; as thou, Father, art in me, and I in thee, that they also may be one in us: that the world may believe that thou hast sent me."[1]

The faith in which we are nearest to the living God, is that which we exercise in meeting God in the Inspiration of the Divine Life, and the highest measure of this faith belongs to this dispensation of the Spirit. But we may not therefore make little account of trust in the living God in a lower region or earlier dispensation. The history of "the cloud of witnesses" is referred to as help to us in running with patience the race that is set before us, and help not superfluous even while we are "looking unto Jesus the Author and Finisher of our faith."[2] We know also that while our highest intercourse with God as the hearer and answerer of prayer—both as to ourselves and in prayer for others—belongs to the eternal life, we are not called to shut out

---

[1] St. John xvii. 21. [2] Heb. xii. 1, 2.

from our minds in such intercourse the lower interests of existence, which it is natural and not sin to feel. No interest which it is *right* for us to cherish is to be held, in this view, "common or unclean." "Be careful for nothing; but in every thing by prayer and supplication with thanksgiving let your requests be made known unto God: and the peace of God, which passeth all understanding, shall keep your hearts and minds through Christ Jesus."[1] And here it is no contradiction to feel authorised to ask God for that which seems desirable, as well as to labour for it, and to feel that we are putting forth a power besides our labour when we so ask because God may grant our request; though as to all but *the absolute good* our asking has a conditional element in it—a reference to God's perfect light. We can believe that our asking is so far a reason with God for granting what, unasked for, God would not have sent, and yet that it may be sometimes higher love to refuse; and that in that case God will refuse. It is peace to be at liberty to go to God presenting our seemingly right desires in the form of requests. It is a part of that peace to know that if what we ask for would be

[1] Phil. iv. 6, 7.

better withheld, it will be withheld. But *waiting on God's decision* is altogether different from waiting to see a necessary flow of events as to which our prayer has had no place as an element in the Divine determination.

No doubt in the measure in which we seek first the kingdom of God our interest in the other things promised to be added thereto will be subordinate, becoming continually more and more so: while—such is the character of the kingdom of God—increased spirituality in our desires will only render the prayers in which these desires utter themselves more earnest. For, although, seeing the glory of God in what we desire more and more clearly, we shall expect it with more abundant assurance of hope, we shall not therefore cease to ask for it—we shall not subside into contemplative and what would be thought more philosophic faith, or content ourselves with passive waiting. Were all our prayers gathered into the Lord's Prayer—and to this prayer tends more and more, as the mind of Christ is formed in us—prayer would still be *prayer*, and *not* simply *praise*. Our attitude in looking forward to the hallowing of the Father's name—the coming of His kingdom —His will being done on earth as it is in heaven—

would be a waiting in the faith that our prayer was hastening what we had prayed for. In this view the thought naturally arises, in remembering the many whose lips in each church service, as well as at other times, repeat the Lord's Prayer, how mighty the power to overthrow the kingdom of darkness and hasten the day of the Lord would be, which would be going forth from the Church were the Lord's Prayer in all lips a prayer in spirit and in truth.

These thoughts on Revelation, Inspiration, and the Kingdom of God within us, will, I trust, be felt to be *practical* in the most important sense of that term. "Seeing that these things are so, what manner of persons ought we to be?" By the path of what God has done from the beginning to make Himself known to men, we are led to the point at which we now stand—the Inspiration of the Divine Life, in this which is distinctively the Dispensation of the Spirit. In the faith of this Inspiration we are able to accept the exhortation, "Keep thy heart with all diligence, for out of it are the issues of life." We respond to the Divine Will in the faith of the Divine Strength, and are quickened with the hope which these words of Christ quicken: "I am the vine, ye are the branches; he that abideth in me and I in him, the same bringeth forth much fruit; for without me ye can do nothing." "I am the living bread which came down from heaven: if any man eat of this bread he shall live for ever, and the bread that I will give is my flesh which I will give for the life of the world." "As the living Father hath sent me and I live by the Father, so he that eateth me even he shall live by me."

That apprehension of the gift of eternal life which in this diversity of form our faith receives, is practical in the highest sense, because through it we are born again of the Will of God: and as the practical power of this light of life is known its claim to be essential light is understood also —the *true* and *absolute* because *spiritual* sense in which we are called to be children of light— seeing light in God's light. Having urged this point on the ground of the very nature of light, I now, in concluding, revert to it—I trust with advantage—urging it on the reader's acceptance on the ground of the provision which God has made for our participation in His light. "Hereby know we that we dwell in Him and He in us, because He hath given us of His Spirit." "God is love, and he that dwelleth in love dwelleth in God, and God in him." Not by development of intellect giving increased capacity of understanding relations of things, nor by clearing the eye of the pure reason for the intuitive perception of absolute truth—however these excellent results may be accompaniments—but by quickening the heart with the divine life of love, does the Spirit of God impart the true and absolute knowledge of God. The words "God is love" we receive in faith as ultimate and absolute truth. Other aspects of the question "What is God?" there are as to which God has not spoken to us—aspects of that question, therefore, on which we may be left in the dark without loss—nay, on which it may well be that we and all creatures are incapable of light—but the certainty with which we know that God is *love*, is as the certainty with which we know that God *is*. We must bless God that it is so: otherwise the one certainty without the other certainty would rack the spirit with hopeless questionings; which yet though hopeless, would be irrepressible, investing the character of God with the infinite interest which to thinking beings must invest the Almighty and Sovereign Lord of the Universe, yet leaving that character in impenetrable darkness. Ours is a solemn time, and deals with questions of unfathomable importance, and we often tremble in taking them up, seeing how earnest minds and minds of a high order are moved by them: and we dare not sin against charity by that hasty solution of a brother's doubts and difficulties which so easily refers intellectual perplexities to moral declination. No one who has taken the beam out of his own eye, will ever be tempted to this cutting of the knot. Ours is a solemn time; but on this rock, "GOD IS LOVE," we can stand as on the Rock of Ages, and while this rock feels firm under our feet, we can bear the shaking of all things. We can use Luther's psalm, "God is our refuge and strength, a very present help in trouble. Therefore will not we fear though the earth be removed, and though the mountains be carried into the midst of the sea."[1] Yea, we can look foward peacefully to what infinitely transcends the trial of Luther's faith—"the removing of those things that are shaken as of things that are made, that those things which cannot be shaken may remain."[2]

[1] Ps. xlvi. 1, 2.   [2] Heb. xii. 27.

But let our certainty here be touched, and where are we? Therefore I feel that, with whatever desire and purpose to subserve the great cause of revealed truth it has been uttered, no word has gone forth to men in this day more full of danger to faith than that which has cast doubt on the possibility of certain knowledge of God. Much acquaintance with the results of lawless and unfettered thought, in which divine Revelation and the individual teaching of the Holy Spirit have been together left out of account, may have led to the endeavour to make men pause by fixing their attention on the instrument with which they have been working in their professed quest of truth, and by shewing its inadequacy for the accomplishment of what they have intended. But though the course of men leaning to their own understanding may well move us to desire to shew them their error and their danger, the history of those who trust in the Lord with all their heart should leave no doubt as to the knowledge of God to which those may attain whom God teaches to know Himself. One aspect of the subject certainly was, "What could men by thinking find out as to God?" But it had this other aspect also, "What of Himself can God by the

Holy Spirit reveal to men?" Surely had the question taken this latter form, the risk would not have been run of limiting God in seeking to humble man.

The conception of a "regulative knowledge" which yet is not absolute knowledge, can have no place if we consider *what that is which is to be regulated.* The will of God as to us is not a will as to our actions, or even as to our thoughts—implying no deeper need than would be met by an answer to the questions, "What are we to do?" "What are we to think?"—the will of God as to us is a will as to *what we are to be*, and is determined by *what God is.* It follows that we cannot know what we are called to be unless we can know what God is. The transition in the mind of St. John from what God is to what we are called to be, and, conversely, from what we are called to be to what God is, illustrates this.[1] To change here the meaning of the word "love" as used in reference to God and to man, is impossible, for this would destroy the Apostle's argument. The very nature, also, of that which God is, and wills us to be, still further determines that here no knowledge can be regulative that is

[1] 1 John iv. 7—16.

not true and certain. God, who is love, wills us to dwell in love. But love in us is to be love to God; and we cannot *love* an unknown God, however we might *fear* Him. If we could conceive of love in man to man leaving God out of account, and if the end of binding spirits thus to each other by a law of love were all that God contemplated—making love to be to them what instinct is to the community of cooperative bees—then God might have left us without the knowledge of what He is, for there would be no practical necessity for such knowledge:—and this is the supposition of those Theists who believe that God is, but do not believe that He invites us to live in the consciousness of a personal relation of love to Himself. But, apart from the fact that God not only is love, but is the fountain of love, and apart from that relation of the second commandment to the first which has already engaged our attention, the will of God, as He has made His will known to us, is just the opposite of such a supposition. We *are* called to love God—to love Him with all the heart and mind and soul and strength: and it is the manifestation of love as it is in God, coming forth to us in Christ, which is represented as revealing love to us, and as making love in us possible.[1] I know the marvellous and merciful contradictions which abound in this region—contradictions between men's systems and their spirits; and that we are not called to judge their spirits, while we must endeavour to take their systems to be tested by what we know as light. Obeying this necessity, it may be our comfort to think that God may be accepting their spirits while He is shewing us what justifies us in condemning their systems. I have endeavoured to justify briefly the condemnation now expressed, and to indicate for the reader's serious consideration the grounds of my solemn conviction, that the question involved is even more important than that of the Inspiration of Revelation. He that could shake my confidence in the Inspiration of Revelation, would indeed rob me of my Bible as I know it—a treasure above all price. But he that could shake my confidence in the certainty of my knowledge of God—what can I say but that he would rob me of my God?

The question now raised as to the possibility of certain knowledge of God is like that as to the existence of God in this respect, that it takes

---

[1] 1 John iv. 9, 10.

us back a step beyond what in a simple and natural state of mind we would of ourselves go. We begin with the assumption that God is to be known as we do with the assumption that God is. Nay, we begin with the assumption of the truth of certain conceptions which we have of God,— as that God is true, that God is righteous, that God is holy, that God is love. Placed as we have been in relation to Revelation, we should find it difficult to say how much of what we believe as to the Divine Character we have learned from the Bible, and how much we might have known without its teaching. How much of its acceptance the Bible owes to light already in man to which it addresses itself, or how far the further light, to the consciousness of which the discoveries of Revelation quicken us, must have remained unattained but for Revelation, we cannot determine. Whatever *might* have been, there can be no doubt as to the actual fact that many, who think they could do without the Bible, owe all that is highest in their mental state to the Bible; and on the other hand, that the Bible would be a gift altogether useless to man but for a light already in man. But the real question is, "However derived that light," in which we say "God is,"

"God is good?" We assume that it is light, and that these statements express what is certainly true: and our anxiety is, not to ascertain their truth, but, assuming their truth, to realise what they express. In this mind we are not inconsistent in complaining of our slowness of heart to believe, or in asking God to help our unbelief. For we are not praying to be enabled to believe something of which as a fact we are doubtful. This, if we consider, we shall see would be a monstrous thought. If the fact is really doubtful it may after all not be a fact, and then it would be loss and not gain to believe it. But our real position is, that we have certain convictions which we do not question, but our understanding and realisation of which we feel to be imperfect, so that they are to us almost as mere words, yet words which we know to express the great realities of existence: and the nature of these realities is such that, in seeking to realise them, we, so to speak, act on the assumption of their reality. In the dim twilight in which we are contemplating them, we are not as persons in a faint light looking out on a dead scene, straining their eyes to see, wishing that they had more light. The realities in our case are not objects of sense, but feelings of the heart of the living God, and forms and acts in which these have been expressed,—and the light in which we are, however dim, is the divine teaching,—and its dimness is because we are slow to receive,—and the will of God to teach and His power to strengthen us to receive are our hope of being taught;—and so we prayerfully open ourselves to the entrance of the living word. Is this or is it not a right mind? Are we to be checked in this path by one saying, "You cannot be sure of what you are assuming; you cannot be sure that these words 'truth,' 'righteousness,' 'holiness,' 'love,' express realities in God, of which your vision though dim is true—as to which therefore it is right to desire a stronger, clearer vision—the filling of the words with their divine meaning." Are we not rather to encourage ourselves by the promise, "they shall be all taught of God," and by the faith of the Inspiration of the Divine Life?

I think I may say, that experience of the fulfilment of the promise of the Comforter—the Spirit of truth who guides to all truth—is *now* chiefly of this character, namely, our having words which express truth, but truth of which our apprehension is dim and shadowy, filled with their spiritual and divine meaning:—a process which from its nature has no necessary limit, but which is not the addition of new certainties to our faith, but our advancing in the true and living knowledge of what we know. We may also have another experience of Divine teaching. We may have our conceptions of the way in which the eternal truth of what God is, is manifested in Christ, modified, and in this sense may come, as to the divine facts which faith embraces, to see what we did not see at one time: as when the faith that Christ died for the elect only gives place to the faith that He died for all mankind. But such a change may be also purely intellectual and not spiritual: and it is most important to realise how strictly in its essence the work of the Holy Spirit, in taking of the things of Christ and shewing them to us, is determined by Christ's relation to us as our life, and is therefore the Inspiration of the Divine Life. That religious truth, while in its substance spiritual, has its suited intellectual form which best clothes it, we do not doubt: but we are constrained to distinguish between the intellectual form and the spiritual substance, by seeing sometimes the most unexceptionable intellectual form held in the absence of the spiritual reality, and, at other times, the unmistakeable presence of the spiritual reality in combination with an intellectual form of thought which is defective, and in part erroneous. In fact, we find diversities in creed which are considerable, apparently making no difference when men awaken to the truth of things, and become quickened with the Divine Life. What might seem the philosophic way of dealing with this difficult but unquestionable fact, would be, to endeavour to ascertain what as to creed is common to all who seem thus quickened; drawing the conclusion, that what is common is that which is essential, and that all besides may be left out of account. But this course would be safe only if the subject were purely intellectual, and if we could conclude from the ideas which men express, what are the real influences telling on their spirits,—which here would be a great mistake. The truth is, that the awakened spirit deals with the living God. Its cry enters into His ears; and the answer is according to His love and to the simplicity and childlikeness—not the intelligence—of its cry. Redeeming love may be more or less truly conceived of; but, if some sense and faith of love be present, the trust in Christ, in whatever darkness cherished, will not be dishonoured. The abiding will of the Father to give his Holy Spirit to them that ask Him, may not be understood; but when the asking is real, and is prompted by felt need, the response is according to the love which is more willing to give than we to ask. As we are baptised into the name of God, the Father, the Son, and the Holy Spirit, so the drawing of the Father to the Son—the Son revealing the Father—this Divine dealing with our spirits in the Holy Spirit is the kingdom of God within us. If it be so, then he who is seeking the kingdom of God—that God in whom he lives and moves and has his being—may be expected to be taught of God in a way which can only be rightly spoken of as *the revelation of God in him:*—a teaching to which all he has heard from without of the will of God to save—of the course and work of redeeming love—of quickening by the Holy Spirit, will be subservient according to what in it has been pure truth of God, and therefore fitted to be used in the Divine teaching; while that which is not spiritual food is left unused. I might illustrate this by reference to the character of the utterances of the full hearts of those, who, having passed out of darkness into God's marvellous light, are declaring their peace and joy in believing, and are calling upon others to "taste and see that God is good." Whatever their intellectual system—be it even the most contracted, and what may have long fettered themselves with questionings of "fixed fate foreknowledge absolute"—there is now with them no question as to the divine love which unbelief is rejecting, or as to divine help which is nigh to every one. They know no love in the Father to which they cannot invite every brother man,— no power to draw near as sons in the Son which is not as free to every one else as to them,—no quickening from the Holy Spirit which they do not believe He wills to put forth in all. They invite others, and they plead with others to have fellowship with them in their fellowship with the Father and the Son; doing this, not in obedience to a system,—as a preacher may offer Christ to all, because he is commissioned and commanded so to do, though his belief is that the reality of Divine Love embraces only a limited portion,— they are free to invite others to drink of the water of life, because they know that it flows freely—because they *find* it flowing freely. It is most instructive to see how intellectual perplexities—difficulties as to prayer, and other difficulties—vanish in actual participation in Divine light,—just as we see no trace of these difficulties in the teaching of the Apostles; the counsel to work out our own salvation being given as a practical exhortation, which is rendered reasonable, not perplexing, by the fact that "it is God which worketh in us to will and to do of His good pleasure."

But while I thus recognise the fact that the Inspiration of the Divine Life reveals Christ in men as the hope of glory, and raises them to communion with the Father and the Son in the kingdom of God within them, and to a true spiritual harmony with the divine constitution of humanity in the Son of God, although they may not be in harmony with that constitution intellectually, and as respects their creed,—I know and feel the great desirableness of that redemption of the whole thinking man which takes place when thought is brought into perfect unison with spiritual truth. I have, indeed, a deep conviction of the possibility of great development of Divine Life in the spirit of a man, while intellectually he is suffered to continue in much darkness as to the counsels of God. The living love in a man is sometimes seen to vindicate its claim to be recognised as flowing from the eternal fountain of love by the universality of its out-flowing —its readiness to serve all—its willingness to die for men in seeking their salvation, even when a most contracted creed holds possession of the intellect: just as we know also, that, on the other hand, it may be that the knowledge which puffeth up may even be the intellectual clearness with which it is seen that charity alone edifieth,—strange as this contradiction may appear. But as the Apostle says, "I will pray with the spirit, and I will pray with the understanding also," so is it right to desire, and prayerfully to wait upon God, that we may attain, not only fellowship in the divine life of love, but also a constantly increasing fellowship in the light of the gracious designs of love. "The ways of the Lord are sought out of all who take pleasure in them."

The manifestly greater freedom with which the Apostles pass from one aspect of truth to another, as compared with what is visible among us—the fact that where we feel a need to be at pains to reconcile, they have no consciousness but of saying the same thing in different forms—this, more than anything else, impresses the conviction, that we have lost somewhat of their light. But in the goodness of God their words remain to us; and it cannot be His will that traditional forms of thought should crust these words to us, obscuring their true meaning. Therefore, while seeking first of all, and above all, a fuller participation in the spiritual light of life in which the Apostles worshipped God in the Spirit, rejoicing in Christ Jesus, and having no confidence in the flesh, we are also to seek deliverance from all that hinders us intellectually from enjoying full participation in their apprehension of divine things. It seems to me, also, that the character of our time makes us to need, and should encourage us to ask, more intellectual light, in order that we may be fully furnished for commending the grace of God to men, and may not, as we may often unconsciously do, put stumbling-blocks in the way of earnest minds by words without knowledge. For who can feel that he is in no danger of so doing, seeing that, all around us, men are equally confident in quoting the words of sacred Scripture in meanings which vary with the varying views of them that quote,—opposite meanings appearing equally clear because of opposite habits of thought? As we pray morally and spiritually, that God may search us and try us, and see if there be any wicked way in us, and lead us in the way everlasting, so is it also right for us to pray for deliverance from such misconceptions of truth as may be intellectually a shortcoming in reference to our high calling as children of the light and of the day, and God's witnesses. Nor will any men be straitened in such prayer, whose peace really flows from the knowledge that God is love, and who can invite God to search out what evil may be in him beyond his own consciousness, *because* he knows the freeness of the grace of God, and that "herein God commendeth His love towards us, in that while we were yet sinners Christ died for us." God "raised Christ from the dead, and gave Him glory that our faith and hope might be in God." He whose faith and hope are in God, rests not on an assumption of perfection in his conceptions of truth, any more than on the measure of his progress in the higher teaching which he is receiving in the school of Christ. He knows God, and peacefully waits for any modification of his thoughts of the divine counsels which increased light may bring. I often feel that there is infinite comfort in the knowledge that "the Comforter" is "the Spirit of truth;" for this implies that the more we know of the truth of things, the more will our comfort abound. In the faith that God is love, we can be patient and peaceful in darkness;—while in that faith we are also prepared to find all additions to our light additions to our joy in the Lord.

> "I'm apt to think the man
> That could surround the sum of things, and spy
> The heart of God and secrets of His empire,
> Would speak but love: with him the bright result
> Would change the hue of intermediate scenes,
> And make one thing of all Theology."
> GAMBOLD.

MACMILLAN AND CO.'S
List of Works adapted for Presents.

ELEVENTH THOUSAND, 18mo. handsomely printed and bound in cloth, 4s. 6d.; morocco, 7s. 6d.; extra, 10s. 6d.

THE GOLDEN TREASURY
OF
THE BEST SONGS AND LYRICAL POEMS IN THE ENGLISH LANGUAGE.

SELECTED AND ARRANGED, WITH NOTES, BY F. T. PALGRAVE,
FELLOW OF EXETER COLLEGE, OXFORD.

Dedicated, by permission, to the POET LAUREATE, with a Vignette after a Design by T. WOOLNER, Engraved by C. H. JEENS.

"No book in the English language will make a more delightful companion than this."—*Spectator*.

Uniform with the "GOLDEN TREASURY."
Third Thousand, cloth, 4s. 6d.; morocco, 7s. 6d., extra, 10s. 6d.

THE CHILDREN'S GARLAND
FROM THE BEST POETS
SELECTED AND ARRANGED BY COVENTRY PATMORE.
With a Vignette after a Design by T. WOOLNER, Engraved by C. H. JEENS.

Uniform with "THE GOLDEN TREASURY."

THE PILGRIM'S PROGRESS
FROM THIS WORLD TO THAT WHICH IS TO COME.
BY JOHN BUNYAN.
With a Vignette after a Design by W. HOLMAN HUNT.

FOOTNOTES FROM THE PAGE OF NATURE;

OR, FIRST FORMS OF VEGETATION.

A POPULAR WORK ON ALGÆ, FUNGI, MOSSES, AND LICHENS.

By the REV. HUGH MACMILLAN, F.R.S.E.

WITH NUMEROUS ILLUSTRATIONS AND A COLOURED FRONTISPIECE.

Fcap. 8vo. 5s.

"Admirably adapted to serve as an introduction to the study of more scientific botanical works, and to throw a new interest over country rambles by bringing into notice the simpler forms of vegetation everywhere to be met with."—*Saturday Review*.

"We earnestly recommend our readers to study for themselves this production, as much for its deep scientific learning as for its strain of true and noble eloquence."—*John Bull*.

GLAUCUS;

OR, WONDERS OF THE SEA-SHORE.

BY CHARLES KINGSLEY, M.A.

RECTOR OF EVERSLEY, AND CHAPLAIN IN ORDINARY TO THE QUEEN.

Containing beautifully Coloured Illustrations of the Objects mentioned in the work. Royal 16mo. elegantly bound in cloth, gilt leaves, 7s. 6d.

"Its pages sparkle with life; they open up a thousand sources of unanticipated pleasure, and combine amusement with instruction in a very happy and unwonted degree."—*Eclectic Review*.

"One of the most charming works on Natural History . . . written in such a style, and adorned with such a variety of illustration, that we question whether the most unconcerned reader can peruse it without deriving both pleasure and profit."—*Annals of Natural History*.

THE
HUMAN HAND & THE HUMAN FOOT.

BY G. M. HUMPHRY, M.D. F.R.S.

LECTURER ON SURGERY AND ANATOMY IN THE UNIVERSITY OF CAMBRIDGE.

With numerous Illustrations. Fcap. 8vo. cloth. 4s. 6d.

"We cordially recommend the book to the public and the profession; the former cannot but be benefitted by it, and the members of the latter, even though accomplished anatomists, will be both interested and amused by the novel way in which many of its points are brought forward. —*Lancet*.

TOM BROWN AT OXFORD.

SECOND EDITION, Three Vols. £1 11s. 6d.

"A book that will live. In no other work that we can call to mind are the finer qualities of the English gentleman more happily portrayed. . . . Mr. Hughes' volumes delight us by the natural manner in which they tell their tale, and not less by their strong and pure English. They are characterised by a manliness of thought which despises affectation, and by that genuine delicacy of feeling which can spring only from a mind exercised in the guardianship of its own dignity."—*Daily News.*

"The extracts we have given can give no adequate expression to the literary vividness and noble ethical atmosphere which pervade the whole book."—*Spectator.*

TOM BROWN'S SCHOOL DAYS.

BY AN OLD BOY.

TWENTY-EIGHTH THOUSAND, fcap. 8vo. 5s.

"A book which every father might well wish to see in the hands of his son."—*Times.*

"No one can read it without exquisite delight, and without being the wiser or the better."—*Notes and Queries.*

SCOURING OF THE WHITE HORSE.

BY THE
AUTHOR OF "TOM BROWN'S SCHOOL DAYS."

WITH NUMEROUS ILLUSTRATIONS BY RICHARD DOYLE.

EIGHTH THOUSAND. Imperial 16mo. printed on toned paper, gilt leaves. 8s. 6d.

'The execution is excellent. . . . . Like 'Tom Brown's School Days,' the 'White Horse' gives the reader a feeling of gratitude and personal esteem towards the author. The author could not have a better style, nor a better temper, nor a more excellent artist than Mr. Doyle to adorn his book."—*Saturday Review.*

PICTURES OF OLD ENGLAND.

BY DR. REINHOLD PAULI.

Translated, with the Author's Revision, by E. C. OTTÉ. With a Map of London in the Thirteenth Century. Crown 8vo. extra cloth, 8s. 6d.

> "Presents the facts of History with the pleasing accessories of a Romance."—*Clerical Journal.*
> "There are some books so admirable, that merely general criticism subsides into, 'Read, it will satisfy you.' Dr. Pauli's work is of this kind."—*Nonconformist.*

EARLY EGYPTIAN HISTORY.

For the Young.

WITH DESCRIPTIONS OF THE TOMBS AND MONUMENTS.

BY THE AUTHOR OF "SIDNEY GREY," &c. AND HER SISTER.

Foolscap 8vo. cloth, 5s.

BY THE AUTHOR OF "RUTH AND HER FRIENDS."

DAYS OF OLD;

OR, STORIES FROM OLD ENGLISH HISTORY.

For the Young.

WITH A FRONTISPIECE BY W. HOLMAN HUNT.

Royal 16mo. beautifully printed on toned paper, and bound in extra cloth, 5s.

> "A delightful little book, full of interest and instruction, . . . fine feeling, dramatic weight, and descriptive power in the stories. . . . They are valuable as throwing a good deal of light upon English history, bringing rapidly out the manners and customs, the social and political conditions of our British and Anglo-Saxon ancestors, and the moral always of a pure and noble kind."—*Literary Gazette.*
>
> "Charming tales of early English history . . . told in a thoroughly healthy and entirely Christian spirit, and are charming alike in conception and expression. . . . This book will make many a young heart glad."—*Freeman.*

SECOND EDITION.

EDWIN OF DEIRA.

BY ALEXANDER SMITH.

Fcap. 8vo. cloth, 5s.

"The Poem bears in every page evidence of genius controlled, purified, and disciplined, but ever present."—*Standard.*

"A felicitous and noble composition."—*Nonconformist.*

"The Poem is almost uniformly good throughout. There are no worthless passages, and very few weak ones. The writer has done his best . . . and the reader's pleasure never flags."—*Morning Herald.*

BY THE SAME AUTHOR.

1. A LIFE DRAMA, AND OTHER POEMS. 4th Edition. 2s. 6d.
2. CITY POEMS. 5s.

BLANCHE LISLE,

AND OTHER POEMS.

BY CECIL HOME.

Foolscap 8vo. cloth, 4s. 6d.

"The writer has music and meaning in his lines and stanzas, which, in the selection of diction and gracefulness of cadence, have seldom been excelled."—*Leader.*

"Full of a true poet's imagination."—*John Bull*

GOBLIN MARKET,

AND OTHER POEMS.

BY CHRISTINA G. ROSSETTI.

With Two Illustrations from Designs by D. G. ROSSETTI.

Foolscap 8vo. cloth.

RAYS OF SUNLIGHT FOR DARK DAYS:

A BOOK OF SELECT READINGS FOR THE SUFFERING.

WITH A PREFACE BY C. J. VAUGHAN, D.D.

CHAPLAIN IN ORDINARY TO THE QUEEN.

Second Edition, handsomely printed with red lines. Price cloth extra 3s. 6d. Morocco old style, 9s.

"The spiritual wisdom and healthy feeling with which these extracts have been selected equally appear in their character, their suitable brevity, and their catholic union of writers of every Christian community. We find thoughtfulness, tenderness, devoutness, strength in the well-chosen extracts."—*Nonconformist.*

ROME IN 1860.

BY EDWARD DICEY, AUTHOR OF "CAVOUR: A MEMOIR."

Crown 8vo. cloth, 6s. 6d.

"Written in plain unaffected English, intent everywhere upon its subject."—*Examiner.*

"So striking and apparently so faithful a portrait. It is the Rome of *real* life he has depicted."—*Spectator.*

"The author writes in a very agreeable and unaffected manner, and shows throughout a creditable anxiety to get at the most reliable sources of information, and to tell the exact truth."—*Saturday Review.*

LIFE AND CORRESPONDENCE OF M. DE TOCQUEVILLE.

TRANSLATED FROM THE FRENCH BY THE TRANSLATOR OF NAPOLEON'S CORRESPONDENCE WITH KING JOSEPH.

WITH NUMEROUS ADDITIONS.

Two Volumes, crown 8vo. 21s.

"The appearance of this work will be welcomed by every politician and every Englishman capable of appreciating exhaustive and solid thought. . . . We do not know another writer unless it be Pascal who leaves precisely the same impression."—*Spectator.*

"Few men of the nineteenth century have attained a more remarkable influence. . . . Charming as specimens of style, they are of infinitely greater value as showing the inner life of a man who was as simple as a child, and yet as gifted as any of the many learned writers and scholars whom France has produced."—*Bell's Messenger.*

MEMOIR OF
GEORGE WILSON, M.D. F.R.S.E.
REGIUS PROFESSOR OF TECHNOLOGY IN THE UNIVERSITY OF EDINBURGH.

By his Sister JESSIE AITKEN WILSON.

With Portrait, 8vo. cloth, price 14s.

"His life was so pregnant in meaning, so rich in noble deeds, so full of that spiritual vitality which serves to quicken life in others; it bore witness to so many principles which we can only fully understand when we see them in action: it presented so many real pictures of dauntless courage and of Christian heroism, that we welcome gratefully the attempt to reproduce it which has resulted in the volume before us. Miss Wilson has entered lovingly upon her task, and has accomplished it well."—*Press.*

In the Press, Crown 8vo.

RELIGIO CHEMICI.
BY GEORGE WILSON, M.D.

THE
FIVE GATEWAYS OF KNOWLEDGE.
A POPULAR WORK ON THE FIVE SENSES.
BY GEORGE WILSON, M.D.

TENTH THOUSAND. In fcap. 8vo. cloth, with gilt leaves, 2s. 6d.

PEOPLE'S EDITION, in Ornamental Stiff Covers, 1s.

THE
PROGRESS OF THE TELEGRAPH.
BY GEORGE WILSON, M.D.

Fcap. 8vo. 1s.

MEMOIR OF EDWARD FORBES, F.R.S.
Late Regius Professor of Natural History in the University of Edinburgh.

BY GEORGE WILSON, M.D. F.R.S.E.

And ARCHIBALD GEIKIE, F.R.S.E. F.G.S. of the Geological Survey of Great Britain.

8vo. cloth, with Portrait, 14s.

"We welcome this volume as a graceful tribute to the memory of as gifted, tender, generous a soul as Science has ever reared, and prematurely lost."—*Literary Gazette.*

"It is long since a better memoir than this, as regards either subject or handling, has come under our notice. . . . The first nine chapters retain all the charming grace of style which marked everything of Wilson's, and the author of the latter two-thirds of the memoir deserves very high praise for the skill he has used, and the kindly spirit he has shown. From the first page to the last, the book claims careful reading as being a full but not overcrowded rehearsal of a most instructive life, and the true picture of a mind that was rare in strength and beauty."—*Examiner.*

The Platonic Dialogues,

FOR ENGLISH READERS.

BY W. WHEWELL, D.D. F.R.S.
MASTER OF TRINITY COLLEGE, CAMBRIDGE.

VOLUME I.

SECOND EDITION. Foolscap 8vo. extra cloth, 7s. 6d.

CONTAINING:

LACHES.	FIRST ALCIBIADES.	MENO.
CHARMIDES.	SECOND ALCIBIADES.	EUTRYPHO.
LYSIS.	THEAGES.	APOLOGY.
THE RIVALS.	CLITOPHON.	CRITO.
	PHAEDO.	

VOLUME II.

Foolscap 8vo. extra cloth, 6s. 6d.

CONTAINING:

PROTAGORAS.	ION.	PHAEDRUS.
GREATER HIPPIAS.	EUTHYDEMUS.	MENEXENUS.
LESSER HIPPIAS.	GORGIAS.	PHILEBUS.

VOLUME III.

Foolscap 8vo. extra cloth, 7s. 6d.

CONTAINING:—THE REPUBLIC, and THE TIMAEUS.

"In the present instance we have most appropriately one of the deepest thinkers of the present day making the Platonic Dialogues as intelligible in an English garb, to the English reader, as they are in the original to himself and the comparatively few scholars. . . . The Dialogues are rendered additionally intelligible, and, indeed, interesting to the English reader, by copious explanatory passages thrown in parenthetically here and there, and sufficiently distinguished from the translated portions by being unaccompanied by the marks of quotation which distinguish the translation throughout. In addition to this, the translation itself merits high praise; while by no means the least valuable portions of the volume are the 'Remarks' at the conclusion of each Dialogue."—*Gentleman's Magazine*.

"So readable is the book that no young lady need be deterred from undertaking it; and we are much mistaken, if there be not fair readers who will think, as Lady Jane Grey did, that hunting or other female sport is but a shadow compared with the pleasure there is to be found in Plato. . . . The main questions which the Greek master and his disciples discuss are not fit simply or theses in Moral Philosophy schools; they are questions real and practical, which concern Englishmen in public and private life, or their sisters or wives who are busy in lowly or aristocratic households. Questions of right and wrong . . . of the virtues which children in National Schools ought to be taught, and the training which educes the best qualities of body as well as mind."—*Athenæum*.

LIFE OF JOHN MILTON,

NARRATED IN CONNEXION WITH THE POLITICAL, ECCLESIASTICAL, AND LITERARY HISTORY OF HIS TIME.

BY DAVID MASSON, M.A.
PROFESSOR OF ENGLISH LITERATURE IN UNIVERSITY COLLEGE, LONDON.

Vol. I. 8vo. With Portraits. 18s.

"Mr. Masson's Life of Milton has many sterling merits . . . his industry is immense; his zeal untlagging; his special knowledge of Milton's life and times extraordinary. . . . With a zeal and industry which we cannot sufficiently commend, he has not only availed himself of the biographical stores collected by his predecessors, but imparted to them an aspect of novelty by his skilful rearrangement."—*Edinburgh Review.*

BRITISH NOVELISTS & THEIR STYLES:

BEING A CRITICAL SKETCH OF THE HISTORY OF BRITISH PROSE FICTION.

By DAVID MASSON. Crown 8vo. cloth, 7s. 6d.

"A work eminently calculated to win popularity, both by the soundness of its doctrine and the skill of its art."—*The Press.*

ESSAYS BIOGRAPHICAL AND CRITICAL:

CHIEFLY ON ENGLISH POETS.

By DAVID MASSON. 8vo. cloth, 12s. 6d.

CONTENTS:
I. SHAKESPEARE AND GOETHE.
II. MILTON'S YOUTH.
III. THE THREE DEVILS: LUTHER'S, MILTON'S, AND GOETHE'S.
IV. DRYDEN, AND THE LITERATURE OF THE RESTORATION.
V. DEAN SWIFT.
VI. CHATTERTON: A STORY OF THE YEAR 1770.
VII. WORDSWORTH.
VIII. SCOTTISH INFLUENCE ON BRITISH LITERATURE.
IX. THEORIES OF POETRY.
X. PROSE AND VERSE: DE QUINCEY.

"Mr. Masson has succeeded in producing a series of criticisms in relation to creative literature, which are satisfactory as well as subtile—which are not only ingenious, but which possess the rarer recommendation of being usually just."—*The Times.*

SECOND EDITION.
GEORGE BRIMLEY'S ESSAYS.

Edited by WILLIAM GEORGE CLARK, M.A.
PUBLIC ORATOR IN THE UNIVERSITY OF CAMBRIDGE.

With Portrait. Crown 8vo. cloth, 5s.

CONTENTS:

I. TENNYSON'S POEMS.
II. WORDSWORTH'S POEMS.
III. POETRY AND CRITICISM.
IV. ANGEL IN THE HOUSE.
V. CARLYLE'S LIFE OF STERLING.
VI. ESMOND.
VII. MY NOVEL.
VIII. BLEAK HOUSE.
IX. WESTWARD HO!
X. WILSON'S NOCTES.
XI. COMTE'S POSITIVE PHILOSOPHY.

"One of the most delightful and precious volumes of criticism that has appeared in these days. . . . To every cultivated reader they will disclose the wonderful clearness of perception, the delicacy of feeling, the pure taste, and the remarkably firm and decisive judgment which are the characteristics of all Mr. Brimley's writings on subjects that really penetrated and fully possessed his nature."—*Nonconformist.*

RUTH AND HER FRIENDS.
A STORY FOR GIRLS.

With Frontispiece. Third Edition. Royal 16mo. cloth, gilt leaves, 5s.

"A book which girls will read with avidity, and cannot fail to profit by."—*Literary Churchman.*

DAVID, KING OF ISRAEL.
A HISTORY FOR THE YOUNG.

BY JOSIAH WRIGHT,
HEAD MASTER OF SUTTON COLDFIELD GRAMMAR SCHOOL.

With Illustrations. Royal 16mo. cloth, gilt leaves, 5s.

"An excellent book . . . well conceived, and well worked out."—*Literary Churchman.*

AGNES HOPETOUN'S SCHOOLS AND HOLIDAYS.

BY MRS. OLIPHANT (AUTHOR OF "MARGARET MAITLAND.")

With Frontispiece. Royal 16mo. cloth, gilt leaves, 5s.

"Described with exquisite reality . . . teaching the young pure and good lessons."—*John Bull.*

OUR YEAR.
A CHILD'S BOOK IN PROSE AND RHYME.

BY THE AUTHOR OF "JOHN HALIFAX."

With numerous Illustrations by CLARENCE DOBELL.

Royal 16mo. cloth, gilt leaves, 5s.

"Just the book we could wish to see in the hands of every child."—*English Churchman.*

LITTLE ESTELLA, & OTHER FAIRY TALES.
BY MAY BEVERLEY.

With Frontispiece. Royal 16mo. cloth, gilt leaves, 5s.

"Very pretty, pure in conception, and simply, gracefully related . . . genuine story-telling."—*Daily News.*

MY FIRST JOURNAL:
A BOOK FOR CHILDREN.

BY GEORGIANA M. CRAIK, AUTHOR OF "LOST AND WON."

With Frontispiece. Royal 16mo. cloth, gilt leaves, 4s. 6d.

"True to Nature and to a fine kind of nature . . . the style is simple and graceful . . . work of Art, clever and healthy toned."—*Globe.*

BROKEN TROTH:

A TALE OF TUSCAN LIFE, FROM THE ITALIAN.

BY PHILIP IRETON.

Two vols. fcap. 8vo. cloth, 12s.

"The style is so easy and natural. . . . The story is well told from beginning to end."—*Press.*

"A genuine Italian tale—a true picture of the Tuscan peasant population, with all their virtues, faults, weaknesses, follies, and even vices. . . . The best Italian tale that has been published since the appearance of the 'Promessi Sposi' of Manzoni. . . . The 'Broken Troth' is one of those that cannot be read but with pleasure."—*London Review.*

THE MOOR COTTAGE:

A TALE OF HOME LIFE.

BY MAY BEVERLEY,

AUTHOR OF "LITTLE ESTELLA, AND OTHER FAIRY TALES FOR THE YOUNG."

Crown 8vo. cloth, 10s. 6d.

"This charming tale is told with such excellent art, that it reads like an episode from real life."—*Atlas.*

ARTIST AND CRAFTSMAN.

Crown 8vo. cloth, 10s. 6d.

"Its power is unquestionable, its felicity of expression great, its plot fresh, and its characters very natural. . . . Wherever read, it will be enthusiastically admired and cherished."—*Morning Herald.*

A LADY IN HER OWN RIGHT.

BY WESTLAND MARSTON.

Crown 8vo. cloth, 10s. 6d.

"Since 'The Mill on the Floss' was noticed, we have read no work of fiction which we can so heartily recommend to our readers as 'A Lady in her own Right:' the plot, incidents, and characters are all good: the style is simple and graceful; it abounds in thoughts judiciously introduced and well expressed, and throughout a kind, liberal, and gentle spirit."—*Church of England Monthly Review.*

MEMOIR OF THE REV. GEORGE WAGNER,

LATE OF ST. STEPHEN'S, BRIGHTON.

BY J. N. SIMPKINSON, M.A.
RECTOR OF BRINGTON, NORTHAMPTON.

Third and Cheaper Edition. Fcap. 8vo. 5s.

"A deeply interesting picture of the life of one of a class of men who are indeed the salt of this land."—*Morning Herald.*

"A biography of rare excellence, and adapted to foster in young minds that sense of duty and spirit of self-sacrifice which are always the attendants of true conversion, but are seldom obeyed and cherished as by George Wagner."—*Wesleyan Times.*

THE PRISON CHAPLAIN;

A MEMOIR OF THE REV. JOHN CLAY,

LATE CHAPLAIN OF PRESTON GAOL.

WITH SELECTIONS FROM HIS CORRESPONDENCE, AND A SKETCH OF PRISON DISCIPLINE IN ENGLAND.

BY HIS SON.

With Portrait. 8vo. cloth, 15s.

"It presents a vigorous account of the Penal system in England in past times, and in our own. . . . It exhibits in detail the career of one of our latest prison reformers; alleged, we believe with truth, to have been one of the most successful, and certainly in his judgments and opinions one of the most cautious and reasonable, as well as one of the most ardent."—*Saturday Review.*

"It cannot fail to charm by its lucid delineations of a character as happily as it was singularly constituted, and of a life devoted with rare constancy and inestimable results to arduous ill-requited toil, in the service of humanity."—*Daily News.*

WORKS BY THE REV. CHARLES KINGSLEY,

CHAPLAIN IN ORDINARY TO THE QUEEN,
RECTOR OF EVERSLEY,
AND PROFESSOR OF MODERN HISTORY IN THE UNIVERSITY OF CAMBRIDGE.

WESTWARD HO!

NEW AND CHEAPER EDITION. Crown 8vo. cloth, 6s.

"Mr. Kingsley has selected a good subject, and has written a good novel to an excellent purpose."—*Times*.

TWO YEARS AGO.

NEW AND CHEAPER EDITION. Crown 8vo. cloth, 6s.

"In 'Two Years Ago,' Mr. Kingsley is, as always, genial, large-hearted, and humorous; with a quick eye and a keen relish alike for what is beautiful in nature and for what is genuine, strong, and earnest in man."—*Guardian*.

ALTON LOCKE,
TAILOR AND POET.

A NEW EDITION.

EXTRACT FROM NEW PREFACE.

"I have re-written all that relates to Cambridge; while I have altered hardly one word in the book beside."

⁎ This Edition will be printed in Crown 8vo. uniform with "Westward Ho!" &c. and will contain a New Preface.   [*Immediately.*

THE HEROES:
GREEK FAIRY TALES FOR THE YOUNG.

SECOND EDITION, with Illustrations. Royal 16mo. cloth, 5s.

ALEXANDRIA AND HER SCHOOLS.

Crown 8vo. cloth, 5s.

THE LIMITS OF EXACT SCIENCE AS APPLIED TO HISTORY.

INAUGURAL LECTURE AT CAMBRIDGE.

Crown 8vo. 2s.

PHAETHON:
LOOSE THOUGHTS FOR LOOSE THINKERS.

THIRD EDITION. Crown 8vo. 2s.

THE RECOLLECTIONS OF GEOFFRY HAMLYN.

BY HENRY KINGSLEY.

Second Edition, crown 8vo. cloth, 6s.

"Mr. Henry Kingsley has written a work that keeps up its interest from the first page to the last—it is full of vigorous stirring life. The descriptions of Australian life in the early colonial days are marked by an unmistakable touch of reality and personal experience. A book which the public will be more inclined to read than to criticise, and we commend them to each other."—*Athenæum*.

RAVENSHOE,

A NEW NOVEL BY HENRY KINGSLEY,

IS APPEARING MONTHLY IN

MACMILLAN'S MAGAZINE.

"One of the best tales now in progress in our periodicals."—*Observer*.

"Ravenshoe will form, when completed, one of the most beautiful novels extant."—*Cambridge Independent*.

CAMBRIDGE SCRAP BOOK.

CONTAINING, IN A PICTORIAL FORM,

A REPORT ON THE MANNERS, CUSTOMS, HUMOURS, & PASTIMES OF THE UNIVERSITY OF CAMBRIDGE.

CONTAINING NEARLY THREE HUNDRED ILLUSTRATIONS.

Oblong royal 8vo. half-bound, 7s. 6d.

UNIFORM WITH THE ABOVE.

THE VOLUNTEER'S SCRAP BOOK.

CONTAINING, IN A PICTORIAL FORM,

THE HUMOURS AND EXERCISES OF RIFLEMEN.

Oblong royal 8vo. half-bound, 7s. 6d.

STRAY NOTES
ON FISHING AND NATURAL HISTORY.

BY CORNWALL SIMEON.

With Illustrations. 7s. 6d.

"If this remarkably agreeable work does not rival in popularity the celebrated 'White's Selborne,' it will not be because it does not deserve it . . . the mind is almost satiated with a repletion of strange facts and good things."—*Field.*

WORKS ADAPTED FOR PRESENTS.

GARIBALDI AT CAPRERA.

BY COLONEL VECCHJ.

TRANSLATED FROM THE ITALIAN.

WITH PREFACE BY MRS. GASKELL,

AND A VIEW OF THE HOUSE AT CAPRERA.

Fcap. 8vo. 3s. 6d. [*This day.*

NEW VOLUME OF

VACATION TOURISTS;

OR,

NOTES OF TRAVEL IN 1861.

The Publishers have much pleasure in announcing that in consequence of the great success which attended the publication of "VACATION TOURISTS FOR 1860," they have made arrangements for publishing a Volume of Tours in 1861. This volume will be edited, like the former one, by FRANCIS GALTON, M.A. F.R.S. The Volume will be ready in the Spring, and will contain, among others, the following :—

I. ST. PETERSBURG AND MOSCOW. By the Rev. ARCHIBALD WEIR.
II. THE COUNTRY OF SCHAMYL. By WILLIAM MARSHALL.
III. THE MONKS OF MOUNT ATHOS. By the Rev. H. TOZER.
IV. THE AMAZON AND RIO MADERA. By the Rev. CHARLES YOUNG.
V. SIX WEEKS IN CANADA. By Capt. R. COLLINSON, R.N. C.B.
VI. A NATURALIST'S IMPRESSION OF SPAIN. By P. L. SCLATER, Sec. to Zoological Society.
VII. GEOLOGICAL NOTES IN AUVERGNE. By ARCHIBALD GEIKIE.
VIII. NABLUS AND THE SAMARITANS. By GEORGE GROVE.
IX. CHRISTMAS IN MONTENEGRO. By I. M.

Cambridge:
MACMILLAN AND CO.
AND 23, HENRIETTA STREET, COVENT GARDEN,
London.

www.ingramcontent.com/pod-product-compliance
Lightning Source LLC
Chambersburg PA
CBHW031831230426
43669CB00009B/1313